A Table in the Wilderness

A Table in the Wilderness

Forty Days of Forgiveness

Thom Rock

RESOURCE *Publications* · Eugene, Oregon

A TABLE IN THE WILDERNESS
Forty Days of Forgiveness

Copyright © 2015 Thom Rock. All rights reserved. Except for brief quotations in critical publications or reviews, no part of this book may be reproduced in any manner without prior written permission from the publisher. Write: Permissions, Wipf and Stock Publishers, 199 W. 8th Ave., Suite 3, Eugene, OR 97401.

Resource Publications
An Imprint of Wipf and Stock Publishers
199 W. 8th Ave., Suite 3
Eugene, OR 97401

www.wipfandstock.com

ISBN 13: 978-1-4982-1825-2

Manufactured in the U.S.A.

All scripture quotations, unless otherwise indicated, are taken from the Holy Bible, New International Version®, NIV®. Copyright ©1973, 1978, 1984, 2011 by Biblica, Inc.™ Used by permission of Zondervan. All rights reserved worldwide. www.zondervan.com The "NIV" and "New International Version" are trademarks registered in the United States Patent and Trademark Office by Biblica, Inc.™

Scripture quotations marked (NRSV) are from the New Revised Standard Version Bible, copyright © 1989 the Division of Christian Education of the National Council of the Churches of Christ in the United States of America. Used by permission. All rights reserved.

Scripture quotations marked (NLT) are taken from the Holy Bible, New Living Translation, copyright ©1996, 2004, 2007, 2013 by Tyndale House Foundation. Used by permission of Tyndale House Publishers, Inc., Carol Stream, Illinois 60188. All rights reserved.

The Qur'anic quotations contained herein are from the Saheeh International translation. Saheeh International, *The Qur'an: English Meanings and Notes,* Riyadh: Al-Muntada Al-Islami Trust, 2001-2011; Jeddah: Dar Abul-Qasim 1997-2001.

To forgiveness pioneers everywhere

We all need to allow ourselves to be led into our own wildernesses, there to be taught what we most need to know, and to be healed where we most need it.

—GERALD MAY

Contents

Acknowledgements | ix

Introduction

The Call of the Wild: A Geography of Forgiveness | 3
Forty Days and Forty Nights: How to Use this Book | 12

The Way of the Open Door

Day One: A Foot in the Door | 19
Day Two: The Unexpected Visitor—Knocking at the Door | 22
Day Three: Lock and Key | 25
Day Four: Across the Doorsill—Stepping Over the
    Threshold | 28

The Way of Walking

Day Five: Put Your Best Foot Forward | 33
Day Six: Where There's a Will, There's a Way | 36
Day Seven: Terra Incognita | 40
Day Eight: Are We There Yet? | 43
Day Nine: One Small Step . . . One Giant Leap | 47
Day Ten: Always One Other | 50

The Way of Perception

Day Eleven: The Oasis vs. The Mirage | 55
Day Twelve: Seeing Is Believing | 58
Day Thirteen: Through the Looking Glass | 62
Day Fourteen: Next Time Won't You Sing With Me? | 65
Day Fifteen: Turning the Page | 69
Day Sixteen: Tongues of Fire | 72

The Way of the Knowing Heart

Day Seventeen: The Heart of the Matter | 77
Day Eighteen: Stone vs. Flesh | 81
Day Nineteen: Forgive and Remember | 84
Day Twenty: It Has a Song, It Has a Sting, Ah, Too, It Has a Wing | 88
Day Twenty-One: Mind Over Matter | 92
Day Twenty-Two: The New Math—Practice Makes Perfect | 96

The Way of the Desert Stream

Day Twenty-Three: The Desert Shall Rejoice and Blossom | 103
Day Twenty-Four: A River Runs through It | 106
Day Twenty-Five: The Water Bears No Scars | 109
Day Twenty-Six: All Is Well | 112
Day Twenty-Seven: Setting Sail—Crossing the Unknown Sea | 116
Day Twenty-Eight: The Opposite Shore | 120

The Way of the Fruitful Field

Day Twenty-Nine: Groundwork—Cultivating Forgiveness | 125
Day Thirty: The Sower Sows the Word | 129
Day Thirty-One: From Single Seed to Bountiful Harvest | 133
Day Thirty-Two: The Wheat from the Chaff | 136
Day Thirty-Three: Allow to Rise | 140
Day Thirty-Four: Bread of Heaven | 144

The Way of the Feast

Day Thirty-Five: Woven Fine—Putting on Forgiveness | 151
Day Thirty-Six: Table Manners | 155
Day Thirty-Seven: A Place at the Table | 158
Day Thirty-Eight: The Full Cup | 161
Day Thirty-Nine: Soul Food—The Pantry of Forgiveness | 164
Day Forty: The Gift of Forgiveness | 168

Afterword: We Live to Forgive | 172

Bibliography | 175

Acknowledgements

EVERY TABLE GATHERING SHOULD include a grace, and when I look up from the feast of words that is this book, I am thankful beyond words for the many precious faces around the table. So many people offered me food for thought, without which my own journey to forgiveness would never have begun. I owe a huge helping of gratitude to David A. Crump, who encouraged me to take my first wavering steps toward forgiveness, and who got the party started in the first place. All I can say is: "*Laissez les bon temps roulez!*"

The party never would have happened without the help of the good people at Wipf and Stock publishers. My sincere thanks go to Justin Haskell, Shannon Carter, Laura Poncy, and especially Matthew Wimer for shepherding the way.

I could not have made this journey without the comfort of knowing I always had a place to rub my sore feet, to rest, and to be nourished. For me that place is the community of Saint Mark's Episcopal Church in Newport, Vermont. I don't know where I would be without your open doors and open hearts. I am especially grateful for the ministry of our bishop, the Right Reverend Thomas Clark Ely, from whom I continue to learn about what it means to ensure that everyone has a place at the table. Indeed, I am thankful for all those in the diocese who saved me a place at their respective tables to explore forgiveness together. Every one of those conversations salted and peppered this book.

To borrow a line from a children's literary classic, "It is not often that someone comes along who is a true friend and a good

Acknowledgements

writer." Somehow, I've been given two such blessings in life: Cam Miller and Sarah Baughman, who kept me on track, helped plan the menu, gave me invaluable feedback, and who made sure the literary spoons and forks were polished.

And, always, to the most adventurous and forgiving person I know, my partner in all things, Jim. Your thoughtfulness, reflections, input, patience, and support have seasoned this book more than you will ever know. I cannot imagine the path or the feast without you.

Introduction

The Call of the Wild

A Geography of Forgiveness

THE MOUNTAINS I SEE outside my window—those I have climbed sometimes for wild berries, sometimes for solace—rise up from the valley below as certain and reliable as a compass. There's no avoiding them. I lift my eyes up to their pinnacled summits nearly every day, their hulking silhouettes visible from just about every corner of town. I watch them change color with the seasons. Chartreuse in spring as their blanketing trees unfurl tender new leaves, they will burn scarlet and vermilion by autumn. Summer twilight can paint them an unlikely combination of saffron and indigo. Come November, if snow hasn't already frosted them crystalline white, they will blow a stormy plum-blue-black. They are a beacon, a symbol of home that I hold to dearly.

Yet climb above their tattered tree lines, where the elements ravage their stony granite caps, and there is suddenly less and less to hold onto . . . until there's nothing left to do but let go. The wind is always hurtling up against those rocky peaks and hiking those final steps is always an exercise in balance and perseverance and in trusting in whatever keeps us from being swept off this earth in the first place: fate, chance, gravity . . .

God.

Walking, especially atop mountains, has also become for me a dynamic image of what forgiveness can look like; a lesson in both moving forward and letting go.

INTRODUCTION

I have always loved wild places. From the wooded trails that led to the fishing and swimming holes of my childhood, to the snow-capped mountains that crown the horizon beyond my window as I write, I have always found, with Thoreau, a quenching tonic in wildness.[1]

There are liminal places, places on the edge, where everything-that-has-ever-been bumps up so abruptly against whatever-might-be that we cannot help but simply be—to be present. In the Celtic tradition such locations are called "thin places," referring to the belief that only three feet separate earth from heaven and the notion that there are places where that distance is even thinner. Places where it is possible to step from one world into another, physical or otherwise. Perhaps even a world such as forgiveness. Most often associated with wilderness, such thin places are almost always uncharted territory: lost rivers, remote mountains, relentlessly empty deserts . . . They have always called to us, quenching our parched souls: "O, that I had wings like a dove!" the psalmist wrote, "I would fly away and be at rest; truly, I would flee far away; I would lodge in the wilderness . . ." (Ps 55:7). The history of human imagination is filled with the promised lands and evocative landscapes of the heart, from Atlantis to Brigadoon to Camelot; from Canaan to Oz to Shangri-La. We're almost always ready to listen to stories about the mysterious, unknown, or unexplored places that elude us on all the usual maps.

But before we answer the beckoning call of wilderness places, before we instill in them some spiritually romantic sense of adventure and discovery, it would prove beneficial to remember that there may be good reason for their uncharted nature; that there is, along with a certain allure, a distinct threat in the depth of any desert, the height of every mountain, and the breadth of any prospect of forgiveness. Invoke the word "wilderness" and certain attributes come to mind: wild, of course, (and sometimes even romantic) but also remote, inaccessible, mysterious, untamed, uncomfortable, unknown—in other words, a place where *we* are definitely not in

---

1. "We need the tonic of wildness," he famously wrote in his classic journal of his own wilderness journey. See Thoreau, *Walden*, 265.

control. Over time, and for good reason, we have learned a healthy apprehension of the wilderness, or at least a distinct hesitancy towards embracing it.

While the wilderness embodies the unknown that is not to say it is formless. To the contrary, "it holds immense refinement and, indeed, clarity," asserted the Irish poet-priest John O'Donohue.[2] In fact, we are inheritors of a long and rich history of leaving the safety of civilization for the wilderness or desert or mountain in order to find answers, to tackle demons, to be tested, to be taught new lessons, or to find transcendence, ourselves, or even God. The wilderness is an ancient, universal experience of tribulation, triumph, and transformation.

There are desert wildernesses and mountain wildernesses and all sorts of variations in between. Some can even delight, such as the light deserts enjoyed by those who dwell far out in the country and away from the always shining streetlamps of cities and suburbs alike. Those wildernesses reveal the full glory of the night sky in all its tinsel and wonder. Other wildernesses, however, are not nearly as welcome, especially those that are as much a state of mind as a physical location. There are any number of metaphorical deserts we may experience in life, both unintended times as well as more intentional moments of aridity: the wide wilderness of grief or depression, the barren desert of loneliness, or even the bitter wasteland of unforgiveness. The stark wildernesses of the spirit or self are what move us most, and have nothing to do with scorching sands or windswept summits. The truest wilderness is far more interior: The desert places of our hearts are what we most fear. While these formations may not loom as large as the actual Sahara or Mt. Everest, they still feel just as impossible to cross or climb, something Robert Frost understood well when he set his poem "Desert Places" in a snowy New England field. We know just the spots the poet refers to. Even if our own desert places are not blanketed with snow, we still recognize the unforgiving landscape: past hurts, shaming or shameful words, guilty or vengeful thoughts, bitter resentments . . . frightfully unforgiving weeds that

---

2. O'Donohue, *Beauty*, 240.

INTRODUCTION

have crowded out anything good or hopeful from the chambers of our hearts. We awake one morning and find ourselves no longer in the garden, but in a vast and very lonely wasteland, "a land where no one travels and where no one lives" (Jer 2:6).

And since our "weeds" are very real to us we tend to them, water them, and take care of them. We are left in a wilderness of misunderstanding unable to imagine, or even believe in the green oasis of forgiveness that waits just over the rise, where "the desert and the parched land will be glad (and) the wilderness will rejoice and blossom, like the crocus" (Isa 35:1). We snuggle in and get comfy on our remote mountaintop, however lonely it may be.

Our desire to remain within safe boundaries and stay the same is a deeply rooted conspiracy. It represents what is perhaps our most tragic mistake in life: that we too often choose to isolate ourselves in the false belief that it will make us safe. It does not make us safe; it only makes us utterly and terribly alone. But thankfully—and by the grace of God—it is possible for us to come to a certain point and say "yes!" to the possibility of forgiveness and forward movement. That moment when we finally give in to the still, small voice whispering long in our ear: "You have stayed long enough at this mountain" (Deut 1:6-7), "Turn, and take your journey." The desert is no place in which to permanently dwell, any nomad can tell you that. But it is into this fear-shaped wasteland that we must venture if we are ever to reach the other side and find our way back to each other. Poets and wanderers have always understood that the best way out is always through, something that the ancient Israelites eventually learned as well, even if they did gripe and grouse along the way. "When Pharaoh let the people go, God did not lead them on the road through the Philistine country, though that was shorter," but instead into and through the wilderness, a desert, to the Promised Land (Exod 13:17; Ps 136:16). Apparently, it was a route that God seems to favor, as we can deduce from a journal entry of the twentieth-century mystic Thomas Merton so many thousands of years later: "I will lead you by the way you cannot possibly understand . . ."[3] But it is exactly

---

3. Merton, *Seven Storey Mountain*, 422.

through this bewildering and incomprehensible way that God reveals who we were created to be. Nowhere is this more evident than in our struggle to arrive at the elusive borders of forgiveness. We think we know the way, having incorporated everything our ancestors thought they knew about forgiving and forgetting, about justice, about apology and about accountability—but still we find the landscape utterly confusing.

The escaping Israelites were equally bewildered by the land; it was not the most direct way and the going was tough. At their lowest, the people grew tired of the journey, impatient for the destination, and complained. They remembered fondly the food they used to eat in Egypt, the cucumbers, the melons, the leeks, the onions, the garlic . . . (Num 11:5). And forgetting that their God had divided the sea and let them pass through it, and had led them with a pillar of cloud by day and a pillar of fire by night, and had split rocks open in the wilderness and gave them drink abundantly from the deep, and caused waters to flow down like rivers, they sniped, "Can God spread a table in the wilderness?" (Ps 78:13–19).

And after all that, *El 'Elyon* their Redeemer did not forsake them, but rather opened the doors of heaven, raining down upon them miraculous nourishment. God spread wide for them an unfailing table in the wilderness; bread fell from the heavens.

Every day.

They called the wonder bread manna, or literally in their tongue, "what is it?" Every day, God provided for them—sustained them—with something they didn't even know of, or comprehend, or even had a name for. I will lead you by the way you cannot possibly understand, indeed.

So, too, God spreads a table in the wilderness for all who hunger for forgiveness: the pilgrim, the curious, the hopeful, the believer, the doubter, the famished. This I know: from the workplace relationship that seems always strained, to the family gathering where childhood hurts bubble up unbidden to the surface decades later, to the relationship betrayed—the unseemly, the unthinkable, the unforgettable—these are the wildernesses where God most lavishly spreads a table in the banquet halls of our hearts.

Introduction

What matters is how we behave at the feast.[4]

I am no expert at forgiveness—believe me—but having experienced its saving grace in my own life and witnessed its power in others, I do consider myself an avid student of just exactly how that grace and power unfolds, and not only because I have found myself needing to ask for forgiveness as often as I have, but also because I have felt both its presence and its absence in my life. Similarly, you may rightly presume if you have read this far, I write not only as a student of forgiveness, and as a lover of wild places, but also as a practicing Christian. I write "practicing Christian" in part because I struggle and marvel, along with C. S. Lewis, that smack dab in the middle of Christianity lays the formidable line: "Forgive us our sins as we forgive those that sin against us." Considering that line Lewis famously wrote, "Everyone says forgiveness is a lovely idea . . . until they have something to forgive."[5]

Jesus was no stranger to the wilderness, whether desert or mountain or any of the many other unknown territories into which he boldly walked. Even though he was led by the Spirit into the wilderness "to be tempted," it was in that solitary place where he ultimately found solace and the start of his public ministry. This is a man who sought out places on the edge, who "would withdraw to deserted places" or go "up the mountain by himself" to pray (Luke 5:16, 6:12; Mark 1:35; Matt 14:23). After one such vigil he came back down the mountain and this is what he said: "You have heard that it was said, 'You shall love your neighbor and hate your enemy.' But I tell you, Love your enemies and pray for those who persecute you" (Matt 5:43–44).

Such baffling and astounding words! Over and over, Jesus is always turning the tables. Sometimes actual ones, as in the recurrent Gospel narrative of the cleansing of the Temple,[6] but more

---

4. This notion is inspired by the Russian writer Boris Pasternak's 1957 New Year's address, "To Friends East and West," in which he wrote that man, "comes as a guest at the feast of existence, and realizes the important thing is not how much he inherits but how he behaves while visiting, what people love and remember him for." See Barnes, *Boris Pasternak*, 331.

5. Lewis, *Mere Christianity*, 115.

6. A narrative that appears in all four of the Canonical Gospels: Mark

often theoretical ones having to do with seeing and doing things completely different from the cultural norm. Another time his friend Peter asked him how often we should forgive others: "up to seven times?" Poor Peter, he probably thought he was being generous! But Jesus said to him, "not seven times, but seventy-seven times" (Matt 18:21–22).

He also knew a thing or two about spreading a table in the wilderness, this Wild One. More than once he provided nourishment for thousands with only a few crusts of bread . . . and in the desert, of all places. Even those closest to him thought it impossible: "How can one feed these people with bread here in the desert?" they asked.

But then, Jesus multiplies.

Echoing the wilderness table of the Hebrew Bible[7] the fifth surah, or chapter, of the Qur'an is titled: "The Table Spread." In it the disciples of Jesus repeat the Israelite's plea: "Can God send down to us a table spread with food from the heaven?"

> They said, "We wish to eat from it and let our hearts be reassured and know that you have been truthful to us and be among its witnesses." Said Jesus, the son of Mary, "O Allah, our Lord, send down to us a table [spread with food] from the heaven to be for us a festival for the first of us and the last of us and a sign from You. And provide for us, and You are the best of providers." (The Qur'an, al-Mā'idah 5:113–114)

And provide, Allah did.

While Jesus—through so many lenses—has so much to teach us about forgiveness, there are many other wilderness guides who've also climbed the mountain, crossed the desert, before us and we will reach out to take hold of their outstretched hands as well: poets and naturalists, as well as mystics and monks, saints

---

11:15-19; Matt 21:12-17; Luke 19:45-48; and John 2:13-16.

7. I use the term "Hebrew Bible" as a more neutral term for the Scriptures that Christians and Jews both read to show respect for a shared biblical heritage, the former "Old Testament" implying that those texts are somehow outmoded and replaced by the New Testament.

INTRODUCTION

and scholars. For, as we shall soon see, there is no single way to our destination; the way is made simply by our walking it.[8] In any unknown land, however, we need all the help we can get. While it is possible to walk that path alone, we're never as alone on the way to forgiveness as we may think we are. There's no telling who one might meet in the desert. The wilderness is where John the Baptizer appeared, proclaiming a baptism of repentance for the forgiveness of sins (Mark 1:4). The opinionated young Pharisee who would eventually come to be known as Saint Paul also journeyed to, and in the wilderness. After his blinding vision of Christ on the road to Damascus he went immediately into the desert of Arabia. When he emerged three years later, he had left behind not only his former name—Saul of Tarsus—but most of his old beliefs as well.

The wilderness changes a person.

While the first Christian monks were not necessarily wilderness sojourners, Antony of Egypt irrevocably linked monasticism with the wilderness in the third century when he deliberately sought out the maddening solitude of the Nitrian Desert in order to draw closer to his God. His earliest followers became known as the desert mothers and fathers—or more affectionately, Ammas and Abbas—and left a wealth of edifying stories and sayings, some of which we will turn to as we also seek out the wisdom of the desert wilderness. Nearer in time, Dr. Martin Luther King Jr. told a gathering in Memphis, Tennessee of his own wilderness journey; that he had "been to the mountaintop. And (that he had) looked over and seen the Promised Land."[9] He wondered whether we would all get there at the same time, but he was absolutely sure of our eventual arrival. Sadly, his question proved telling; he stepped bleeding onto those elusive shores without us the very next day.

Poets too are no strangers to the wilderness; some, like Frost and O'Donohue, we've already met. But we're sure to bump into a few others as we make our way across the desert. Ultimately, it is the wilderness itself that is, perhaps, our greatest teacher. Whether

---

8. A sentiment we shall visit repeatedly during our wilderness journey, and inspired by the title poem in Machado, *There Is No Road*, 55.

9. King, *A Call to Conscience*, 222–23.

traversing desert plain or mountain peak there's only so much baggage you can slog along with before you realize you really don't need to carry it around anymore. It doesn't matter what we bring with us into the wilderness of forgiveness so much as what we leave behind.

Forty Days and Forty Nights
How to Use this Book

MY HOPE FOR THE volume you hold is that it may lead you, over a period of forty days and nights, to a place where forgiveness seems possible. My prayer is that it will bring you to a moment where forgiveness becomes not only possible, but irresistible.

Our wilderness journey into forgiveness is divided into daily readings and reflections. These are revealed to us through sacred texts as well as nonreligious voices. The readings and reflections are intended to be thought-provoking and to be explored either alone or with a partner, or even in a small group. However you choose to travel, might I make the suggestion of keeping a notebook or journal with you for recording your thoughts, insights, and questions over the next forty days?

While the following meditations are organized thematically and each theme in turn fits roughly into the time period of a week, I do not at all mean for this particular structure to portray our journey through the wilderness to forgiveness as being that sequential or linear. I encourage you, the reader, to feel free to adopt the mystic's motto, "the desert knows neither time nor space" and adapt this structure to meet your needs, spending time with each day's readings and reflections whenever and as best fits wherever you are in your life right now. It goes without saying that you need not wander in an actual desert or retreat to some remote wilderness in order to make this trek. God meets us wherever we are on the journey to forgiveness.

Whether climbing a mountain or traversing a desert, successful sojourners gather their gear ahead of time: a helpful trail map, an accurate compass, a dependable lantern . . . checking and double-checking for readiness. For extensive climbs and crossings a base camp is set up from which to head out each day. Consider this book your base camp. From it you will head out into your own wilderness places to explore another peak of the mountain—to gain yet another vista of forgiveness—and to it you may return each evening after each day's journey. Your trail map is the combined wisdom of our wilderness guides, with whose words you will begin each day. Your heart, along with your willingness to embark on this quest and your intention to complete it, will be your sure and reliable compass.

Why forty days and forty nights? Why not thirty or seven or three-hundred sixty-five? References to the practice of forty-day wanderings are seemingly ageless and cut across history, cultures, and religions. Just as the ancient Israelites wandered in the wilderness, and Christ went into the wilderness to pray and get clear about his ministry, and Muhammed received his commission in a wilderness cave, the number forty also abounds in all three Abrahamic faiths, and as we will see, many other traditions as well.

It is said that Muhammad was forty years old when he first received the revelation of the Qur'an delivered by the archangel Jibril, or Gabriel. Later, he would spend forty days praying and fasting in a cave. The Prophet Ibrahim is said to have endured and survived forty days in a fire because Allah made the flames to be like flowers. Similarly, the Prophet Yunis, known to Jews and Christians as Jonah, was inside the great whale for either three or forty days, depending on which translation you read. Devout believers who devote themselves to God Almighty for forty days are promised springs of wisdom breaking forth from their hearts and flowing from their tongues.

It is also said, in one old Arabic proverb, that in order to truly understand a people, you must live among them for forty days. "The further you go into the desert," says another, "the closer you come to God."

Introduction

The number forty is mentioned well over a hundred times in the Bible and travels not only throughout the Tanakh and the New Testament, but also throughout the Talmud, the ancient and authoritative compendium of Jewish civil and ceremonial law and customs. It is repeatedly associated with the power to increase or lift up, to purify, or to renew. For example, the Talmud teaches that when someone has become ritually impure, they must cleanse themselves in a *mikveh*, a ritual bath which must be filled with forty measures of water. That measure of water is meant to recall the story of Noah and the great flood, when the earth was purified by forty days and forty nights of rain. The one emerging from such a *mikveh* is considered as pure as the world was after those flood waters subsided—an image that travels forward in time to, and is closely attuned with, John the Baptist waist deep in the River Jordan baptizing penitents.

Additionally, after the ark came to rest—on a mountaintop, no less—Noah waited another forty days before opening the window and sending out first the raven, then the dove (Gen 8:6). Arriving on the shores of another Promised Land generations later, Moses sent out his own birds to scope out the place (Num 13:17-18). At the end of forty days the spies returned bearing grapes and pomegranates and figs, saying "we went into the land to which you sent us, and it does flow with milk and honey! Here is its fruit" (Num 13:27). Still later, the mighty Goliath took his stand against the Israelites twice a day, morning and evening, for forty days before the Philistine met his match in David (1 Sam 17:16). The prophet Jonah warned the people of Nineveh that in forty days their city would be overthrown, and the people of Nineveh used those forty days for prayer and repentance and were saved (Jonah 3:4,10).

It seems Moses made more than one trip up the mountain, where he would stay—as did Muhammed in his cave—for forty days at a time and return with face all aglow (Exod 24:18, 34:28-29; Deut 10:10). Those to follow would also repeat this fortyfold practice down through the ages. It is said that the prophet Elijah fasted for forty days and forty nights on his journey to Mount Horeb, the same mountain where God gave the law to Moses, after being fed an angelic meal that gave him the strength to travel those forty days to that mountain of God (1 Kgs 19:8).

Jesus himself also fasted for forty days in the wilderness immediately after his baptism in the Jordan.[1] Any number of saints have replicated this time period as a means of battling demons or communing with their God, from Benedict to Patrick to Thomas Merton. Once, near the end of his life, Saint Francis of Assisi made one final forty day retreat on Mount Alverna. It is said that he so desired to be like Jesus that he received the stigmata there, returning to his beloved brothers pierced by God's love.

The number forty appears to have significance across cultures. In a story that intensely mirrors that of Jesus' time in the wilderness, the ancient Mesoamerican deity Quetzalcoatl fasted for forty days as well, during which he was tempted by the devilish Tezcatlipoca. Egyptian mythology relates the desert story of the conflict between Horus and Set, a forty day struggle that was believed ultimately to have unified Lower and Upper Egypt. The founder of Sikhism was deeply influenced by forty days of prayer. Many prayers in Hinduism consist of forty *dohas*, or stanzas. And according to some versions of the story, the Buddha attained enlightenment after forty days of fasting and meditating beneath the Bodhi Tree.

There is one more forty day period that comes to mind and one that overflows with promise: After his suffering and crucifixion—at which he forgave his executioners—Jesus showed himself to the apostles and provided many convincing proofs, appearing to them during forty days and speaking about the wonders of the kingdom to come (Acts 1:3). And after their Beloved was finally lifted up and taken from their sight, the apostles stepped off that mountain called Olivet, setting off for a new and an eternally changed world.

---

1. A time period that observant Christians still replicate in observing Lent with forty days of fasting, service, and study, and into which this book neatly folds: If you should choose to journey into the wilderness as a Lenten experience, the first day's reading would fall on Ash Wednesday, the last day's reflection on Holy Saturday, allowing for a weekly pause from the book each Sunday following the tradition that Sundays are not considered fasting days.

INTRODUCTION

The period of forty days represents a period of struggle and of testing. It denotes a kind of preparation for whatever is to follow. Put another way, it is a time of grace—for what follows is always a period of restoration, of hope, and of promises fulfilled. That is ultimately all we need and all that really matters in the desert: God's promise, set down and awaiting us like a table in the wilderness. Forty days . . . forty nights . . . forty ways to find our way to forgiveness . . . We may not know now just exactly how we'll get there—we don't need to. Yet we can believe without doubt that we will arrive, and when we arrive, that there is a place set and waiting for each and every one of us at that table.

The Way of the Open Door

DAY ONE

A Foot in the Door

See, I have placed before you an open door that no one can shut.
—REV 3:8

If one were to give an account of all the doors one has closed and opened, one would have to tell the story of one's entire life.[1]
—GASTON BACHELARD

WE SELDOM TAKE NOTICE of the many doors we pass through each day, but many are the portals we come in to and go out from as we go about our daily routine. Doors are double agents; when open they are welcoming invitations, yet when closed they become symbols of mystery or even separation. They keep out and they keep in, admit and deny, separate and connect. A door can be a boundary marker and a door can be a passageway to somewhere else, an entrance or an exit. An open invitation or—well, a door slammed in one's face. We put out the welcome mat by our front door, or we hang a "do not disturb" sign on its doorknob. We "show someone the door" when we want to be rid of them, we

---

1. Bachelard, *The Poetics of Space*, 224.

try to "get a foot in the door" when we have even bigger hopes, and we comfort each other with that old cliché, "when one door closes another one opens." We come in the front door, sneak out the back door, twirl our way through revolving doors, and trip over trapdoors. And that's not even taking into consideration the many metaphorical doors of our curiosity, imagination, and memory. "How concrete everything becomes in the world of the spirit when an object, a mere door, can give images of hesitation, temptation, desire, security, welcome and respect."[2]

There's no getting around it; doors are our agreed upon ways in or out. And in opening them we open ourselves too, especially when the door opens inwards, as in the case of forgiveness. "Be an opener of doors," wrote the poet and transcendentalist Ralph Waldo Emerson, in his journal almost midway through the nineteenth century.[3] It remains sage advice as we begin our wilderness journey today. When we ask ourselves, "What might my life look like if I could forgive, or if I were forgiven?" we crack open the door to forgiveness just a little bit more than it was before. And if you're not yet ready to crack open the door, that's okay, too. But at least draw back the curtain and take a peek outside the window and consider the view.

The thought of actually turning the doorknob ever so slightly until the faint sound of the latch bolt disengages, and the imminent prospect of the door swinging open on its rusty old hinges—not to mention the thought of who or what we might find on the other side—all too often keeps us from grabbing on to the door handle at all. Perhaps because we know deep down somewhere that whoever opens a door is never quite the same being as the one who closes it behind them. Instead of opening the door to forgiveness we schlep instead all the way across town to bitterness and resentment's place—they share a duplex owned by their cousin anger—and park our sorry butts down on the doorstep content to stay there, invited or not, for as long as it takes for You-Were-Right

---

2. Ibid.
3. In Crothers, *Ralph Waldo Emerson*, 29.

and I-Was-Wrong to come skipping down the sidewalk holding hands.

The irony, of course, is that You-Were-Right and I-Was-Wrong are constantly tripping over each other's feet and seldom arrive intact, if at all. But even more importantly, Forgiveness' door wasn't ever locked in the first place. In fact, God had left it slightly ajar, waiting for us to open it and come walking through. The pivotal question becomes whether or not we approach that open door with an equally open heart and mind.

We have such a vast treasure of forgiveness and compassion and empathy in our hearts. We only need to open the door to discover it. We can open our hearts to the world without even opening our doors, the Tao Te Ching reminds us. And so let today be the day you open the door of your heart to forgiveness. Pay careful attention to the doorways you pass through today; the details of what distinguishes one from the next, the firm archways that hold them open, the hinges that glide and swing open or shut either silently or with a creak. The way your hand grasps on to a doorknob and the way your arms and shoulders assist your fingers. Take note of how your physical movements of entrance might be not unlike the transformational thoughts of entering into the possibility of forgiveness. Be aware that when you approach a door you prepare to leave something behind as surely as you move beyond wherever you are right now. Opening doors today, notice whether or not your head automatically nods in a gesture of welcome, or your posture reveals some other emotional orientation; write forgiveness "on the doorframes of your house and on your gate" (Deut 6:9). Do this until a door opens in the center of your heart.

Today we reflect on the thought that in the wilderness there are doorways that invite us to other worlds everywhere. Those doors, including the entranceway to forgiveness, are within each of us.

DAY TWO

The Unexpected Visitor
Knocking at the Door to Forgiveness

Knock upon yourself as upon a door, and walk upon yourself as a straight road. For if you walk on that path, you cannot go astray; and when you knock on that door, what you open for yourself shall open.

—SILVANUS

She knocked and waited, because when the door was opened from *within*, it had the potential to lead someplace quite different.[1]

—LAINI TAYLOR

THE PROPHET ELIJAH, a heroic figure in Jewish tradition—and no stranger to the pages of the New Testament and the Qur'an as well—is honored and remembered each year at the Pesach Seder, the feast that marks the beginning of the Jewish holiday of Passover. Tradition holds that a special cup of wine is to be placed on the seder table and the door of the house opened, both actions in honor of Elijah who, according to prophesy, will arrive one day as an unknown guest to "herald the advent of the Messiah."

---

1. Taylor, *Daughter of Smoke and Bone*, 33.

The Unexpected Visitor

Whether or not Elijah will extend the courtesy of knocking on the door before entering remains a mystery, but countless children have opened and closed the door to their house and then run excitedly back to the cup to see if the level of the wine had altered—to see if the prophet of old had, indeed, come in.

At his lowest point in life, Elijah prayed "enough, already!" and sat down by a scrubby brush in the wilderness to die. But an angel came to him and fed him a cake baked on hot stones and gave him water to drink, and strengthened by that singularly angelic meal, he travelled forty days and forty nights to Horeb—"the mountain of God"—where he holed up in a cave for the night. Now it seems that God was out for a walk that night and Elijah was surprised to suddenly hear God speaking to him. God walking on earth is quite something and, well, the wind started to pick up and blow, breaking pieces of rock off the mountain's side, and the ground shook, and the earth burned as if on fire. Elijah assumed that God, being so powerful, was surely in all that wind and shaking and burning. But God was not in the wind. And after the wind God was neither in the earthquake, nor after the earthquake in the fire.

"... And after the fire came a gentle whisper" (1 Kgs 19:11–12).

There are more than a few ways to knock on a door, from the polite tap to the full-fisted pounding that announces urgency. But if we're in another room we might not hear the knock, no matter how loud or urgent it may be. So we've invented brass doorknockers and chiming doorbells to announce unknown visitors and welcome guests alike because hearing the knock or rap or chime is a primary and critical step in opening any door. But equally important is *listening for* that knock, as we do when we are expecting a beloved friend or family member at our door any minute.

Forgiveness, like God, does not necessarily arrive like a howling wind or crashing earthquake or blazing fire but—after the fire—as a "gentle whisper." Boris Pasternak, the author of that timeless love story, *Doctor Zhivago*, wrote in a letter to his muse and real-life Lara, Olga Ivinskaya, "when a great moment knocks on the door of your life, its sound is often no louder than the beating of your heart and it is very easy to miss it."[2] Let's face it, life can get noisy; there are plenty of ding-dongs out there to distract us. But we can slow down, take a deep breath, and pay attention to the steady beating of our heart—to listen carefully for how forgiveness might arrive unexpectedly at our door. And when we do, forgiveness might just stealthily slip through the door invisible like Elijah in the night.

"Ask, and it will be given to you; seek, and you will find; knock and the door will be opened to you," the Matthean gospel tells us (7:7). And somehow, that door is both a passageway and the destination, the invitation and the door prize—the promise of prayers answered. And somehow that door is our own hearts that we are knocking on.

Listen! Today forgiveness knocks at your door.

Only your hands can open it.

---

2. In O'Donohue, *To Bless the Space*, 4.

DAY THREE

Lock and Key

Though the doors were locked, Jesus came and stood among them and said, "Peace be with you!"

—JOHN 20:26

Then there were doors that wouldn't open unless you asked politely, or tickled them in exactly the right place, and doors that weren't really doors at all, but solid walls just pretending.[1]

—J. K. ROWLING

"Make not your thoughts your prisons," the Bard of Avon cautioned in his tragedy, *Antony and Cleopatra* (act 5, scene 2). And yet we do . . . all the time, especially when it comes to forgiveness. We say, "Oh, I'll forgive them—as soon as they apologize." We insist that we were right and "they" were wrong, and therefore conflate forgiveness with condoning. Our thoughts naturally dwell on the unforgettable and mistranslate that word into the unforgivable. Or, so hemmed in by our own guilt, we convince ourselves that we are not worthy of being forgiven. We close the door to our hearts tightly and bolt and double-bolt it

---

1. Rowling, *HarryPotter*, 137.

from the inside; the click and glide of cold metal against cold metal, and then an eerie quiet but for the sound of our own frightened breathing.

We might even go so far as to say that the state of unforgiveness is not unlike Egypt in the time of the Israelites; a land of servitude and enslavement, bondage and bitter herbs. What we desperately need is our own exodus story, our own journey through the wilderness. Further still, while it might be possible to dismiss the story of the Israelites as just another dusty old tale that the ancients told each other around the campfire, the fact remains that "Egypt," "Pharaoh," and "Promised Land" easily remain potent and resonant metaphors on the journey we find ourselves, of the longed for location of our heart, and of all that holds us captive in our own lives here and now.

Sadly, and much too often, we become accustomed to the safety and predictability of those prison walls. Until, thanks be to God, the day when that misidentified comfort no longer comforts and we recognize our primal longing to be liberated. More often than not, questions are what liberate us. But knowing the right question to ask is not always immediately evident. "How can I ever escape from this prison?" we ask ourselves. How *do* I forgive? How much will it cost? How long will it take? How many times must I forgive? And because we don't know how—or cannot even imagine an answer to it—we repeat the question over and over, and in every imaginable way, never stopping to think that, in fact, "how?" might not even be the right question. It's not the only choice, after all. There's "What if . . .," for example, or even "Why not?" Or maybe the question and the answer to all of the above is simply saying "yes" to the *possibility* of forgiveness in our lives. Or, if not yet "yes," then at least a hearty "maybe."

Above all we should, as Rilke so tenderly advised, try to live our questions themselves. "Don't search for the answers," he wrote to a young aspiring poet, "which could not be given to you now, because you would not be able to live them. And the point is, to live everything. Live the questions now. Perhaps then, someday far in the future, you will gradually, without even noticing it, live your way into the answer."[2]

In the Muslim faith there are ninety-nine "most beautiful names" for Allah. One especially seems fitting here: *al-Fattâh*, "the One who opens what is closed, the Revealer, the Easer of all that is locked." The Buddha is said to have asserted, "I am the door." Similarly, in the Johanine gospel, Jesus announces that he is "the gate" or, as some translations put it, "the door" (10:9). Locked doors posed no problem for Jesus either. Although his disciples closed themselves behind locked doors out of fear after his crucifixion, Jesus came in to the room and stood among them, saying, "Peace be with you!" A week later he repeated the door-defying reminder (John 20:19; 26). And later, when his apostles were imprisoned for teaching in his name an angel of God staged a night-time prison break by opening their locked doors, leaving the officers who were sent to fetch them the next morning scratching their heads and saying, "We found the jail securely locked, with the guards standing at the doors; but when we opened them, we found no one inside" (Acts 5:23).

It's okay if we sometimes feel like we just don't have it in us to get up and unlock the door. There is always One who can still open our locked doors and stand with us in our hurt and fear, and walk with us in our doubt and apprehension.

We may think we can padlock our hearts and throw away the key. But this I know: God knows the combination.

---

2. Rilke, *Letters to a Young Poet*, 34.

DAY FOUR

Across the Doorsill

Stepping Over the Threshold of Forgiveness

Across the doorsill the breeze at dawn has secrets to tell you. Don't go back to sleep![1]

—JALAL AL-DIN RUMI

In desert and mountain wilderness, people discover liminal places suggesting thresholds between where they have been and where they are going.[2]

—BELDEN C. LANE

AN IN-BETWEEN PLACE, THE threshold has long been regarded as embodying great power. In the third century, the ancient Greek philosopher Porphyry declared the threshold to be a sacred thing, an assertion that visionaries, mystics, poets, prophets, seers, fools, and shamans have understood for centuries as they moved with poise and surety over and back through the thresholds of body, mind, and spirit. From Rumi's delight at the doorsill

---

1. Barks, *The Essential Rumi*, 36.
2. Lane, *The Solace of Fierce Landscapes*, 38.

to John O'Donohue whispering in our ear: "You can trust the promise of this opening; unfurl yourself into the grace of beginning . . ."[3] to countless others, these teachers not only bring back the light of truth and hope and possibility, but more importantly, they endure the fire of staying in that place in-between in order to hold it open for us, so that we too may pass through into such possibility. Whether or not the threshold seems to us a sacred space, it can still become a beginning place as we wait within it, and look beyond it to the path beyond.

Originally referring to the doorway that led to the place where grain was threshed after it was harvested, where oats or wheat or barley were sorted, sifted, and separated from husk or straw or chaff, the word *threshold*, as the ancients understood, has a way of accommodating so much more than that simple meaning. Our common definition today includes the dividing material that forms the bottom of any door of any room or building. We step over and through such physical thresholds every day. But we've also come to use the word to describe a crossing over not only from place to place but from time to time as well; we say we are on the threshold of a new era . . . of discovery, or technology, or some other shift. So too the word is used to denote the level or point at which something will change: if our level of income rises above a certain threshold, for example, we can expect our tax rate also to alter. Similarly, in the realm of our bodies and minds we say someone has a relatively high or low "pain threshold" to mean the point at which a physiological or psychological sensation or effect begins, the point at which we become aware of and begin to feel a certain pain or discomfort.

Today we stand on another kind of threshold, an in-between place, a thin place . . . a place of decision. Step over this threshold and we are on a journey, a crossing which holds out the promise of change—of changing everything. Standing in the doorway we are faced with a choice: will we put on our sturdy hiking boots and set out into the wilderness beyond? Or will we ignore the poet's call,

---

3. From his blessing prayer, "For a New Beginning," in O'Donohue, *To Bless the Space*, 14.

and go back to sleep, and miss out on all the secrets the morning breeze has to tell us?

We can linger in this place between before and after as long as we need; in fact we should, for it is more than just a physical divider between inside and out, as well as more than an imaginary or symbolic line separating one reality from another. The threshold is a point of departure and also one of entry, of transformation—of beginning something new and becoming someone new. To ask ourselves before venturing off what we're willing to leave behind, what patterns of thinking and behavior have prevented us from crossing this threshold before, and what might help us over it now are important and vital considerations. In other words, are we prepared to leave behind the old sneakers that no longer serve us well even if they still feel comfortable—to set down for the time being our old ideas about justice and accountability, about forgiveness and reconciliation? Have we filled our canteens with curiosity, packed intention and an open mind into our backpack?

But we mustn't linger too long at the doorsill either; it is much too tiny to contain the truth of who we really are, and as any traveler knows it's easier to discern the path before us in the light of day. The point is to be as awake and aware as possible of our decision, and of how the weight of the body can shift and roll from first the heel to the ball of the foot and then to the toes—how hips and legs and soles of feet all work together to carry our thoughts and hopes and desires across the threshold. The sensation of one foot lifting up off the ground and moving forward, the movement of the leg as it swings through the air like a prayer.

The Way of Walking

DAY FIVE

Put Your Best Foot Forward

As shoes for your feet put on whatever will make you ready to proclaim the gospel of peace.

—EPH 6:15 (NRSV)

You have brains in your head. You have feet in your shoes. You can steer yourself in any direction you choose.[1]

—DR. SEUSS

IN ANCIENT MYTHOLOGY WINGED shoes were all the rage; for fashionable young gods no other footwear would suffice. Sure, they were fleet and made one light-footed beyond compare, but the way they highlighted the turn of ones ankle, the strength of one's calves . . . well, it was enough to make both mortal and god swoon. Perseus used winged sandals to help him on his journey to slay the merciless Medusa; Mercury and Hermes both donned a pair to navigate between the worlds of the divine and the mortal—the landscape of the soul.

---

1. Geisel, *Oh, the Places You'll Go!*

The Way of Walking

Try as we might, we haven't yet succeeded in reproducing the ancients' flying footwear, although over time mere humans have developed quite a variety of foot coverings, from the practical to the stylish to the pointedly absurd. We have shoes for walking, shoes for running, shoes for dancing and—well, shoes for just about anything. From high heels to high tops, sling backs to slippers, clogs to crocs to clodhoppers, we've got our feet covered. We even cover our coverings when it gets too wet or slushy with rubber galoshes or Wellies.

We wouldn't think of dancing a ballet in steel-toed work boots, or running a marathon in stilettos. Likewise, we need the proper footwear for our journey to forgiveness. While the Israelites wandered through their wilderness most likely in the common footwear of their time—sandals—we probably shouldn't consider walking to forgiveness in our flip-flops or bedroom slippers. We need to strap on something that will provide excellent traction, give us a good foothold, the support that we'll need: a sensible shoe that will allow us to make sense of the wilderness into which we tread; one that will allow us to step steadfastly into forgiveness.

Maybe even something with a wing.

We are, in a very real way, carried through life by our shoes. We trustingly place our feet in them each morning day after day. Sometimes they even do seem to allow us to fly, as when we are swept up in a moment of great joy or sheer tenderness. They run us to the store to pick up milk and they walk us down the aisles of our most meaningful moments. Still other times they march us straight into difficult territory. In the classic film, *The Wizard of Oz*, Dorothy "inherits" a pair of magical ruby slippers after her house accidently lands on their previous wearer, a wicked witch. They slip easily onto her feet and fit her perfectly. At the end of the film one last power contained in the ruby slippers is revealed to Dorothy: that they can swiftly return her to Kansas if she simply clicks her heels three times and repeats those now immortal words, "There's no place like home." But there are no ruby slippers in life and certainly not along the path we're on, even if it is our true home to which we are walking. Forgiveness doesn't always fit at first and seldom slips right on. The concept doesn't come easily to us. We may, in fact, need a shoehorn to squeeze our stubborn hooves into forgiveness the first few times.

Even though we are meant to walk in forgiveness it still might gall and pinch at first like a new pair of shoes. As the saying goes, "he whose boot pinches thinks the world too narrow." Our soul work is not that much different than any sole work; just as all footwear requires some maintenance and getting used to, so too does forgiveness. Most hikers know that the best way to break in a new pair of boots is to try them out for brief periods of time, slowly wearing them for longer and longer bits as they feel more and more comfortable. The same is true for any shoe. Polishing can soften the leather and make it suppler if they are persistently stiff. A shoetree can ease and maintain the necessary structure and form. The trick is to keep up with the stretching and polishing before everyday scuffs and scratches have a chance to turn into something more lasting.

Putting on shoes today, you are trying on forgiveness. Notice how your feet feel, how the arch supports your foot, and the inner sole absorbs the weight of your body as you step forward. You don't need to imagine walking a mile in forgiveness' shoes, just take a few steps. Go ahead, walk over to the mirror and see how forgiveness looks on you.

DAY SIX

Where There's a Will, There's a Way

Whether you turn to the right or to the left, your ears will hear a voice behind you, saying, "This is the way; walk in it."

—ISA 30:21

Your path is straight ahead of you. Sometimes it's invisible, but it's there. You may not know where it's going but you have to follow that path . . . It's the only path there is.[1]

—CHIEF LEON SHENANDOAH

NOT ONLY DID ISAIAH proclaim that there is a way no matter which way we turn, he went on to say that a clear way in the wilderness is already prepared for us; that God finds in the desert a direct highway to our hearts (Isa 40:3). A similar way can be found in Islam where it is taught "Allah may forgive for you what proceeded of your sin and what will follow, and complete His favor upon you and guide you to a straight path" (The Qur'an, al-Fath 48:2). One of the principle teachings of the Buddha is the Noble Eightfold Path, a way that is said to lead to the cessation of suffering and to self-awakening.

1. In Harvey, *The Direct Path*, xi.

Where There's a Will, There's a Way

Scripture is full of examples of multiple ways or passages from one place to another, from the long desert journey of the Israelites, to the Magi's pilgrimage to Bethlehem, to a solitary tentmaker's life-changing trip from Jerusalem to Damascus—from Saul to Paul—and his later willingness to pull up every tent peg of his life and set out on a journey to follow Jesus. Or Muhammad's great Night Journey astride the magnificent steed Buraq accompanied by the archangel Jibril—or Gabriel—on a single evening in 621 CE. According to The Qur'an and other supplemental writings about the life of Muhammad, the winged Buraq brought the Prophet to seven heavens where he met first Adam, then Jesus, Joseph, Enoch, Aaron, Moses, and Abraham, and finally ascended to *al-Bait-al-Ma'mur*, the House of Allah, where he received instructions on the details of prayer to take back to the faithful (The Qur'an, al-Isrā' 17).

The one who would become known as the Christ was also familiar with pathways and passages; indeed, Jesus walked an awful lot. From Nazareth in Galilee to the temple in Jerusalem, from the River Jordan to the Judean Desert—where he conducted his own forty-day journey in the wilderness—and back to Galilee and a wedding feast at Cana; in fact, throughout Galilee and Capernaum and Samaria, and even beyond the shores of the Sea of Galilee to the land of the Gerasenes, to Caesarea Philippi and Mount Herman and back to Jerusalem, by way of Jericho and Bethany and the Mount of Olives, to the garden of Gethsemane and on to Golgotha. Jesus walked. No wonder Paul, along with the earliest Christians, was so comfortable with the invitation to pull up the tent pegs, and to set out on a journey, to be called a "Follower of the Way," to listen and respond to Jesus' outrageous call, "Come, Follow me" (Matt 4:19; Mark 1:17).

We can walk ourselves into our best self, our best thoughts, according to the Danish philosopher Søren Kierkegaard, who wrote that there is "no thought so burdensome that one cannot walk away from it . . . Thus, if one just keeps walking, everything will be all right."[2] To put it another way, we ought to be on the

---

2. Kierkegaard, *The Essential Kierkegaard*, 502.

The Way of Walking

way instead of constantly getting in our own way. Or in the words of that good ol' Western trailblazer Louis L'Amour, "The thing to remember when traveling is that the trail is the thing, not the end of the trail. Travel too fast and you miss all you are traveling for."[3] A way is a guide and not necessarily a fixed path even if we come across a place where those before us have walked many times in the same spot. We each have our own path to forge to forgiveness; each step isn't always self-evident and, contrary to what some would have us believe, our steps to forgiveness do not unfold in a certain or sequential manner.

There is a wonderful moment in the Arthurian legends when all the knights were gathered around the Round Table. The Holy Grail (which the knights believed was the blessed cup Jesus used at the Last Supper) showed itself to them, although not in its full glory but covered with a shining cloth, and then disappeared. Arthur's nephew Gawain proposed a quest: that all there gathered go in search of the Grail "to behold it unveiled." And thinking it unbecoming to journey forth as a group, "each entered the Forest Adventurous at that point which he himself had chosen, where it was darkest and there was no path."[4] Likewise, we enter the forest of forgiveness at that point which we ourselves choose. Where there is a path it is left by some other wayfarer and is not ours. Your own footprints are the only path, nothing else. The important thing is not the road you take, but the road you make.

Sometimes the way to forgiveness *is* apology, or even remorse or restitution, although those are seldom the only ways and certainly not always. More often the way to forgiveness is simply a desire for things to be different from the same-old, same-old sameness of unforgiveness, or what Saint Augustine referred to as "divine discontent." Sometimes the way to forgiveness is an increased sense of awareness and attention, or an unwavering intention. If we are lucky the way to forgiveness is a simple shift in perspective. With work, the way to forgiveness can be an increased

---

3. L'Amour, *Ride the Dark Trail*, 53.

4. A legend addressed in much more detail in Campbell, *Pathways to Bliss*, xxix.

capacity for compassion. And, mercifully, the way to forgiveness can sometimes simply be the passage of time or, inexplicably, the gift of grace unfolding in our lives. Again, it doesn't really matter *how* we get there so much as that we say "yes" to the destination.

There may be more than one way to forgiveness, but there's only one way to find out for sure: "Strive for the greater gifts," Paul wrote to the Corinthians, "and I will show you a still more excellent way" (1 Cor 12:31, NRSV).

DAY SEVEN

Terra Incognita

Stand at the crossroads and look, and ask for the ancient paths, where the good way lies; and walk in it, and find rest for you souls.
—JER 6:16

When you come to a fork in the road, take it![1]
—YOGI BERRA

THE UBIQUITOUS "FORK IN the road" is yet another moment of decision that shows up at various points along any journey. Read almost any story and you're sure to come across at least one character facing a certain crossroad moment in his or her life. Sometimes we find ourselves at one of those wilderness crossroads as in Dante's classic *Inferno*, "midway upon the journey of our life," and standing in a dark wood. Other times we're more like Lewis Carroll's young Alice in Wonderland, wondering which way to go in a place that just makes no sense. If we think carefully about the interaction she has with the Cheshire Cat there is much wisdom in it:

---

1. Berra, *When You Come.*

Terra Incognita

> "Would you tell me, please, which way I ought to go from here?" asked Alice. "That depends a good deal on where you want to get to," said the Cat. "I don't much care where," said Alice. "Then it doesn't matter which way you go," said the Cat.[2]

On an expedition as important as the one we've embarked upon everything depends on paying careful attention to "where we want to get to." Of course, Alice's response, "I don't much care where," is a sadly familiar one. How often we slide through life not much caring which way we're headed or trudging mindlessly down familiar paths. As the saying goes, "if you don't change direction, you may end up where you're heading."

The word *intention* will be important at every fork in the road we come to along the path to forgiveness. We ought to care very much indeed where we're going and keep that care at the forefront of our thoughts every day of our wilderness journey. Otherwise we will find ourselves once again down the back alley of blind bitterness or the rocky road of resentment, or some other well-worn way of unforgiveness. Those ways will try their best to tell us that nothing's changed since last we were there. But something *has* changed. We've realized that unless we're willing to embrace and explore more unfamiliar paths, we can only expect a steady wearing away of our very selves until there's nothing left. We're bound and determined to avoid the hazardous path, as the scribe penned ages ago, to "not stumble at [the same] obstacle twice" (Sirach 32:20, NRSV). Our old friend Robert Frost reminded, in the concluding lines of what is perhaps one of his most recognized poems, that being intentional about the steps taken at any fork in the road—taking the less-traveled pathway—is not only paramount, but often makes all the difference.[3]

The Hebrew Bible puts that difference bluntly: there is one road that leads to life and another that, although it may appear to be right, in the end leads only to death (Prov 12:28; 14:12). Standing at the crossroads we must look around us and be clear about

---

2. Carroll, *Alice in Wonderland*, 52.
3. See "The Road Not Taken" in Frost, *The Poetry of Robert Frost*, 105.

where we want to go. To ask, with the prophet Jeremiah, for the ancient path to forgiveness and redirect our wayward selves to "where the good way lies" and claim it, and walk in it as if our very life depends upon it.

While some directions and decisions are clearly right or wrong, there are others that can be far less clear. Forgiveness, for example, quite often seems more like a fairy tale than an ancient sacred path, more like a fictional place that exists somewhere over the rainbow and only in the imagination. There will always be that voice in the back of our minds wanting to confuse us into inaction or wrong action, saying first, "that way is a very nice way..." and then, unhelpfully, "but it's pleasant down that way, too," as the Scarecrow tells a confused Dorothy at yet another literary—and cinematic—fork in the road. All too often we look down the yellow brick road of forgiveness and, shaking our heads, turn and head the other direction back into the cornfield. Regardless of what our heads are stuffed with, scratchy misconceptions or simply straw, deciding which path to take isn't entirely up to our brains anyway. When it comes to forgiveness we need to be more like the Tin Man and think with our hearts. Only then will we ever find our way back home.

DAY EIGHT

Are We There Yet?

The wilderness takes us beyond our expectations into God's surprises.[1]

—JOHN LIONBERGER

Therefore I tell you, whatever you ask for in prayer, believe that you have received it, and it will be yours.

—MARK 11:24

IN MY NECK OF the woods, there is a saying long tossed around by ol' timers, but still invoked today as a funny but somewhat true statement: "You can't get there from here." Well, more accurately the "you" is rarely vocalized and the R's fall by the wayside, leaving what usually sounds something like "Can't get they-ah from hee-yah," in the local vernacular. The expression is not meant to relay that there is literally no way, but rather that there is no direct or easy route from point A to point B. Sometimes forgiveness can feel just as inaccessible. There are still roads around here that slowly fade from paved highway to dirt road to nothing more than two tire tracks running through the woods, the space

---

1. Lionberger, *Renewal in the Wilderness*, v.

between them overgrown with goldenrod and grasses, only to simply disappear altogether into the wild green wilderness. If there is a decent road it's likely to travel "the long way round," winding its way over a mountain or two, or some distance downstream where the only river crossing is, or all the way around the long shoreline of the lake. Or even all of the above. But there is a way. The same might be said of forgiveness: sometimes, it requires going what seems a long distance out of the way in order to arrive at its location.

Mark Batterson points out that although it is in our human nature to want to get from point A to point B "in the shortest amount of time and by the easiest route possible . . . getting where God wants [us] to go isn't nearly as important as becoming who God wants [us] to be in the process."[2] We do not want to take our eyes off the destination, but that does not mean we should neglect paying attention to the process of getting there and who we are in that process—to be awake to and aware of our feelings, our past hurts and our present resentments, how our memories color our daily being regardless of accuracy, and what our intentions are regarding this journey. The danger is to spend so much time dwelling on where we have been or where we are supposed to be going that we haven't a clue where we actually are right now. Perhaps a better question to ask isn't so much "Are we there yet?" but rather "Are we *here* yet?"

The important thing is to not let our expectations get in the way. Just as the road to hell is paved with good intentions, the way to forgiveness is all too often paved with expectations. We owe, perhaps, that original expression to Saint Bernard of Clairvaux (1091–1153), who is thought to have said, "Hell is full of good wishes and desires." And before that, Virgil noted in his *Aeneid* that: "It is easy to go to hell" (*facilis descensus Averno*). Expectations can be just as hellish; they assume certain outcomes by certain ways and allow very little room for any change of course. We may believe that our particular road to forgiveness is paved with good intentions, but we should tread carefully. More often than

---

2. Batterson, *Wild Goose Chase*, 137.

not those cobblestones are really just expectations in disguise: expectations of what forgiveness entails, what forgiveness really looks like, and what it requires. We squander so much time and too many opportunities living in expectation, in waiting for "The Apology," or in needing to be right, or wishing things were different from the way they are.

Released of those expectations it may feel and appear to us, and to others, that we are merely wandering about with no clear path in mind. But there can be a certainty to wandering the ancient path we are on. Saint Augustine's assertion that to search for God is to have found God holds true for our quest as well. To search for forgiveness is, in a way, to have found forgiveness. When we so much as attempt to say yes to forgiveness—or even desire to say yes—forgiveness is somehow somewhere present to us even if we do not immediately recognize it. Or as Bilbo whispers to Frodo at the Council of Elrond in Tolkien's *Lord of the Rings* trilogy, "Not all those who wander are lost; the old that is strong does not wither, deep roots are not reached by the frost."[3] Henry David Thoreau, who found the wilderness to be like a tonic, had much to say about walking as well, or as he preferred to say, sauntering. In his essay *Walking*, published posthumously, he gives a useful history of that word, praising those who have a natural affinity for sauntering:

> ... which word is beautifully derived "from idle people who roved about the country, in the middle ages, and asked for charity, under pretense of going *à la sainte terre*"—to the holy land, till the children exclaimed "There goes a *sainte-terrer*", a saunterer—a holy-lander ... This is the secret of successful sauntering. He who sits still in a house all the time may be the greatest vagrant of all, but the Saunterer, in the good sense, is no more vagrant than the meandering river, which is all the while sedulously seeking the shortest course to the sea.[4]

---

3. Tolkien, *The Fellowship of the Ring*, 193, 278.
4. Thoreau, *Walking*, 2–3.

The Way of Walking

Today we practice being saunterers in the land of forgiveness, keeping in mind that the longest journey *à la sainte terre* is often the interior one, even as the sea of forgiveness pulls us surely home.

We are journeying to the holiest of lands today; we are holy-landers.

DAY NINE

One Small Step . . . One Giant Leap

See, I am doing a new thing! Now it springs up; do you not perceive it?
—ISA 43:19

Every moment is a new arrival, a new bestowal . . . The cardinal sin is in our failure not to sense the grandeur of the moment.[1]
—ABRAHAM JOSHUA HESCHEL

An old Irish proverb says, "a good beginning is half the work." But beginnings are stealthy; they begin to begin long before we ever see any signs of their having begun. Saint Frances de Sales encouraged patience in all things, but chiefly patience with our selves—a task he noted, that required beginning anew every day. Benedictine monks and nuns have embraced for centuries the Rule of St. Benedict which contains the following four simple yet gracious words: "Always we begin again." The desert father, Abba Poemen said about Abba Pior that every single day he made a fresh beginning.[2] Abba Moses asked Abba Silvanus, "Can a man

---

1. Heschel, *The Wisdom of Heschel*, 51.
2. Nomura, *Desert Wisdom*, 1.

lay a new foundation every day?" The old man said, "If he works hard he can lay a new foundation at every moment."[3] The wilderness through which we travel is a place of unceasing beginnings, of endless first steps.

No matter how far we stray from forgiveness, there is always an invitation to begin again. To build a new house in which forgiveness might dwell. Not just each day, but each moment offers us the chance to lay a new foundation that upholds and transcends our daily work. The mystery of forgiveness is perhaps never quite finished, and as we endeavor to discover the foundations of forgiveness we also embrace ever-new possibilities of what shape its as yet unfinished house might look like.

All beginnings are hard. But a house is built step by step, and room by room, and in a certain order. Sure, there are different ways to build a house, but we would not expect to raise a roof without first having built a foundation and walls to support it; to have an attic before a cellar. "In the attic it is a pleasure to see the bare rafters of the strong framework . . . the carpenter's solid geometry,"[4] the French philosopher Gaston Bachelard wrote so eloquently. But before we can ever admire that geometry we must first dig down deep and excavate the ground beneath it, and pour a solid foundation. And, "when it comes to excavated ground," Bachelard concluded, "dreams have no limits."[5]

We tend to look at forgiveness as a complete and imposing structure, a magnificent mansion or palace, or all too often as a temple. We add room after unnecessary room onto forgiveness, but when it comes right down to it all forgiveness really asks for is something much simpler, like a hut or lean-to. Despite their humble and meager accommodations, the desert fathers knew a thing or two about these things. Abba John the Little said: "No one can build a house from the top down; rather you build the foundation first and then build upwards." And when people questioned what he meant by that, the monk clarified: "The foundation means

---

3. Keller, *Desert Banquet*, 34.
4. Bachelard, *The Poetics of Space*, 18.
5. Ibid.

your neighbor . . . and [one] ought to start from there. For all the commandments of Christ depend on this."[6]

Suddenly the simple hut isn't that simple.

Fortunately, we are not the first forgiveness pilgrims, but inheritors of a wealth of knowledge and experience from those who have gone before us. The notion from the rabbinic tradition that, while we are not called upon to complete a task before us, we are not free to evade it is one such pearl of wisdom. The Benedictine grace—always we begin again—is another. In other words, in order to make the world a better place we must start the task ourselves without despairing that we cannot accomplish such an overwhelming prospect. At times it seems like forgiveness is more than we can muster. Our forgiveness forebears encourage us from afar not to give up and remind us that all we need to do is to begin and try our best, and to be kind to ourselves when we fall. Our attempts at forgiveness may not be perfect; in fact, they probably won't be. Chances are we will not get forgiveness right the first time, or the time after that—or the time after that. But that doesn't mean that we shouldn't even try, that we are free to evade it. We do not start by shingling the roof. We begin by laying a cornerstone, and then another and another and another, until we have a firm foundation on which to build.

"This, however, is our hope: God will redeem where we fail, [and] complete what we are trying to achieve."[7]

---

6. Nomura, *Desert Wisdom*, 46.
7. Heschel, *God in Search of Man*, 407.

DAY TEN

Always One Other

You know when I sit and when I rise; you perceive my thoughts from afar.

—PS 139:2

Walking, I am listening to a deeper way. Suddenly all my ancestors are behind me. Be still, they say. Watch and listen. You are the result of the love of thousands.[1]

—LINDA HOGAN

BENEATH CLOUDS OF IMPENDING war the three-masted *Endurance* set sail for the Antarctic in the summer of 1914 under the watchful eye of her captain, Sir Ernest Shackleton. The ship would never return. Beset by and ultimately crushed in the polar ice floes, it broke up and sank below the icy waters of the Weddell Sea in November of the following year. But her crew, in what is surely one of the greatest survival stories of all time, did return. Stranded on drifting pack ice hundreds of miles from land with no means of communication and with limited supplies, the crew of that expedition ultimately survived hundreds of days before

---

1. Hogan, "Walking," 14–16.

making their first landfall on Elephant Island in the South Shetlands and from where a rescue mission began.

Less than a decade later the poet T. S. Eliot would publish one of his most important poems, *The Waste Land*, part of which was inspired by the story of how, at their most trying moments the crew of the *Endurance* repeatedly felt that there was one more member of the company among them than could be actually counted. It is, of course, also a reference to the story in the Lukan gospel of two disciples encountering, although not recognizing at first, the Risen Christ along the road to the little village of Emmaus (24:13–32).

Long before the road to Emmaus or the remarkable sea journey of the *Endurance*, King Nebuchadnezzar of Babylon had a similar experience (Dan 3). Being king he thought himself omnipotent and set up an image of gold to be worshipped by all, under penalty of being thrown into a blazing furnace. Nowadays we might say the king was a bit of a control-freak, question his hold on reality, and ignore his megalomaniacal decree. But in ancient Babylon folks wouldn't dare say nor do such a thing. Except they did—well, at least three did. Shadrach, Meshach, and Abednego, devout Jews living under the rule of ol' Neb, steadfastly refused to serve the king's gods or worship his image of gold. Naturally, they were summoned before the king and their allegiances questioned. When it became clear that their allegiance was not with the king he grew furious and ordered them to be tied up and the infamous furnace heated seven times hotter than usual. And so the three were bound and thrown into the blazing fire:

> Then King Nebuchadnezzar leaped to his feet in amazement and asked his advisers, "Weren't there three men that we tied up and threw into the fire?" They replied, "Certainly, Your Majesty." He said, "Look! I see four men walking around in the fire, unbound and unharmed, and the fourth looks like a son of the gods" (Dan 3:24–25).

These stories remind us that whatever the nature of our journey, whether it is through mountain or desert, a wilderness of fire or ice or even unbelief, we are never as alone as it might seem at the time. There is always one other walking beside us.

The Way of Walking

Not only are we never alone on our journey, but our companion guides also ensure that we can see where we're going along the way. They are a lamp to our feet and a light to our path (Ps 119:105). Further still, our destination is already being prepared by them for our eventual arrival. "My Father's house has many rooms," Jesus said: "If that were not so, would I have told you that I am going there to prepare a place for you? And if I go and prepare a place for you, I will come back and take you to be with me that you also may be where I am. You know the way to the place where I am going" (John 14:2–4).

The word most often translated as "room" in that rather well-known passage is the Greek word *monai*. But the King James Bible translated it differently: "In my Father's house there are many *mansions*," and other translations, such as the New Revised Standard Version anglicized the word as "dwelling place." The word does have to do with abiding in a certain place, but certainly nothing neither as opulent or magnificent as what the word mansion conjures up, nor as narrow as the four walls of a single room. Some translators would say that this abiding is not so much about permanently dwelling, but another kind of stopping: a temporary halt along the way—that *monai* is more like a resting place or a wayside shelter or even a park bench where a sojourner might rest a while on his or her journey.

We are pilgrims on a pilgrim road. Today we pause and reflect on our pilgrim hearts, knowing that we are never alone on the journey.

The Way of Perception

DAY ELEVEN

The Oasis vs. The Mirage

I will turn the desert into pools of water, and the parched ground into springs.

—ISA 41:18B

Faith is an oasis in the heart which will never be reached by the caravan of thinking.[1]

—KAHLIL GIBRAN

IN THE WILDERNESS OUR eyes can deceive us. If Jesus and others have gone ahead of us to prepare a resting place along the way, we ought to be sure of that wayside shelter; or in other words, to know the difference between an oasis and a mirage. To be sure, an oasis is a place of replenishment, a place to slake your thirst: quenching and soothing and comforting. When one comes upon water in the desert, one comes upon nothing less than life itself. An oasis is the perfect place not only to rest but also to reflect upon the journey so far, a fertile spot along the desert way. At an oasis we pause to replenish provisions and to visit with those

---

1. In Miller, *Thoughts from Earth*, 8.

also taking a break beneath the refuge of the broad fronds of the desert palms. The oasis is a place to stop and think about where we have come from—to reacquaint ourselves with the stumbling blocks we have put in our way in the past—and where we are going. All too often, wanting to be sure of where we're headed simply prevents us from heading anywhere at all. But the oasis offers a chance to pop a sweetmeat into our mouth, lean back in the shade, and maybe even get over our embarrassment for once and ask for directions to the next resting place along the way.

Curiosity, stillness, intention, wisdom, perspective, faith . . . each of these offers a particular kind of shade. Even, perhaps especially, discomfort can be an oasis if we acknowledge its living waters. The challenge is to recognize the reality of an oasis when we see it, and not dismiss it as a mirage. Yet, the comfortingly cool and leafy green enclosure of any oasis can also be seductive, tempting the sojourner into not just a temporary rest but something more lasting, in which case it becomes not an oasis but surely a mirage. It is certainly wise to rest along the way, but we must not mistake the welcome oasis for the Promised Land and get too comfortable, stay too long. It's tempting to stop at an oasis for good, to say to ourselves, "my feet are sore and this is further than I've ever come before" and give up.

But, like water, when we cease to move we become stagnant. "The man who never alters his opinions," wrote William Blake "is like standing water, and breeds reptiles of the mind."[2] The mirage implies a figment of the imagination, a misperception where the oasis fades away and we realize it was only a mirage. But there are mirages that are more fade-resistant than others and yet still are not oases but more like swamps. A holy curiosity can be a rejuvenating oasis, but if we ask ourselves the same sticky question over and over (how? or, why me? for example) that oasis becomes neither rejuvenating nor a figment of our imaginations—a mirage—but a very real and indelible swampland for our soul.

The trouble with stopping along the way is that our minds, in fact, do not stop with us: eventually our crocodilian thoughts

2. Blake, *Complete Poetry and Prose*, 42.

The Oasis vs. The Mirage

will rise up from those murky waters. The mosquitoes of self-righteousness, bitterness, and revenge, having furtively bred in the swampland of our furtive rumination, will buzz unmercifully in our ears, and will not be content until they suck away every hope of moving forward. The old proverb, still waters run deep, is commonly understood to mean that beneath a placid exterior hides a passionate nature. But perhaps its closest equivalent in French says it even better: *Il n'est pire eau que l'eau qui dort* (no water is worse than quiet water).

More often than not, the real work of forgiveness isn't so much to discern the oasis from the mirage, but living waters from the swamp.

DAY TWELVE

Seeing is Believing

Those who think they know something do not yet know as they ought to know.

—1 COR 8:2

In the wilderness your . . . preconceptions cannot protect you. Your logic cannot promise you the future. Your guilt can no longer place you safely in the past. You are left alone each day with an immediacy that astonishes, chastens, and exults. You see the world as if for the first time.[1]

—LAWRENCE KUSHNER

JESUS WAS ALWAYS MAKING up all kinds of stories. Truth be told, he never met a simile he didn't like. Consummate storyteller that he was, for him everything was always like something else: a lost coin or a tiny seed; wheat, or leaven, or weeds; a pearl of great price or a wedding feast; a door, or gate, or the eye of a needle. People would ask him questions and he would say, "The kingdom of God is like . . ." and then off he'd go into another one of his stories. "In case you didn't get that," he'd say barely catching his

---

1. Kushner, *Honey from the Rock*, 22.

breath, "I'll tell you another one." And off he'd go again. The pattern surely must have grated on the disciples' nerves; according to Matthew they even questioned him about it outright. "Why do you speak to them in parables?" they asked. "Stories speak to the heart not to the mind," he answered them. "I speak in parables because most people do not see that salvation is all around them even though they have eyes with which to look yet do not see, ears with which to listen but do not hear, and minds with which to think yet do not understand." And then he added affectionately, "But blessed are your eyes because they see, and your ears because they hear" (Matt 13:16). Of course, we know that the disciples didn't really get what he was saying but they nodded their heads anyway, inwardly pleased at the compliment from their beloved teacher and too embarrassed to say, "From your lips to God's ears!"

The fact is that, though we depend upon our eyes and ears to help us make sense of the world, they all too often deceive us. Perhaps that's why prophets and prosecutors have long cautioned against judging only by what our eyes see and making decisions based solely on what our ears hear (Isa 11:3). Even after his execution and resurrection, the disciples of Jesus still didn't trust their own eyes and ears when he showed himself to them. They thought he was the gardener, for goodness sake, or some vagabond walking along the dusty road to the little village of Emmaus, and at least one of them would only believe the apparent apparition was in fact Jesus if he could put his finger into the wounds left behind by the cross: irrefutable proof.

The problem is that there is no such thing as immaculate perception. What our eyes routinely see is consistently colored by memory and hope and perspective and preconception and misconception—by whatever we tell ourselves that we believe. Ironically, our vision is really like a kind of blindness, always intercepted by our preconceived notions of what is real and what is not, of what we think we know. We believe we know a scene simply because it feels familiar and that we therefore grasp its entire meaning and relevance. This is not a parable or a metaphor or a simile. We have an actual blind spot, exactly where our retina and optic nerves engage in a rhumba of reflection and observation, and every day our brains tell us little white lies to make up for that dance. This comes as no surprise to some: "eyes are blind," the Little Prince says in Antoine de Saint-Exupéry's classic story by the same name, "you have to look with the heart."[2] We can see so much more when we look with more than our eyes—when we allow, for example, our hearts to glance Godward. It is said that when asked if there was anything worse than being blind Helen Keller quipped, "Having no vision."

With the millions and millions of optical cones and rods that make up our sense of sight, our very eyes, we can detect varying degrees of light and a whole spectrum of colors. Why then is it so difficult when it comes to forgiveness to say what we see, what it looks like? In the realm of science critical observation is not a definitive, one-time declaration but a careful and continuous process of looking—and then looking again. The naturalist Joseph Wood Krutch noted that "In nature one never really sees a thing for the first time until one has seen it for the fiftieth."[3] Similarly, we cannot truly see or know forgiveness for the first time until we hold it up and look at it from every possible angle.

The Talmud teaches that we do not see things as *they* are; we see things as *we* are. Who knows if the American naturalist and writer Henry David Thoreau ever read those words of the rabbinic fathers, but ages hence he wrote similarly of his one room experiment at Walden Pond that "things do not change; we change."[4] He saw the world differently after his own journey in the wooded wilderness. He went to those woods because he wished to live deliberately and with intention, to remove himself from the way things were in his world. What he found instead was that the only way to change the way things were was to alter the way in which he saw them.

2. Saint-Exupéry, *The Little Prince*, 71.
3. Krutch, *The Desert Year*, 4.
4. Thoreau, *Walden*, 349.

Seeing is Believing

No matter what we might have thought forgiveness was like in the past we look at it with fresh eyes today.

DAY THIRTEEN

Through the Looking Glass

Anyone who listens to the word but does not do what it says is like someone who looks at his face in a mirror and, after looking at himself, goes away and immediately forgets what he looks like. But whoever looks intently into the perfect law that gives freedom, and continues in it—not forgetting what they have heard, but doing it—they will be blessed in what they do.

—JAS 1:23–25

Reflection comes between us and every other person and object in the world. An object or a person can be reflected in so many ways.[1]

—JOHN O'DONOHUE

IN ONE OF THE famous fairytales told by the Brothers Grimm there is a magic mirror that a vain and evil queen kept in her castle. "Mirror, mirror on the wall, who is the fairest one of all?" she would ask, expecting the usual and complimentary response. Every day the mirror would reply, "You are the fairest of them all." Until, that is, the fateful day when the mirror's reply altered: "Famed is thy beauty, Majesty, but hold, a lovely maid I see. Rags

---

1. O'Donohue, *Four Elements*, 74.

cannot hide her gentle grace. Alas, she is more fair than thee." The jealous queen, as we know, determined to get rid of her competition, Snow White. A poison apple did the trick, provided a sleeping death that could only be reversed by "love's first kiss."

Enter Prince Charming.

It's a delightful fairytale, but only that.

To be fair, though, there's a bit of the evil queen in all of us. We ourselves consult multiple mirrors every day, those made of glass and silver as well as certain people in our lives or even social values and expectations that we look to in order to reflect back to us who we think we *should* be. But none of these ever reflects back to us our true or entire being and they are, each of them, destined to distort in some way, like the fun house mirror at a carnival or even the backwards reflection offered in the rearview mirror of any car. There are even two-way mirrors. Sometimes a mirror can be water cupped in the hand at the edge of some beautiful and idyllic lake or stream. But then the wind ripples the surface and the reflection is twisted into some other shape. The spirit in the evil queen's mirror could only tell the truth, but most mirrors twist and stretch and contort the truth in some way all the time.

At the same time, we live in a hall of mirrors, one that constantly casts back to us a disorienting array of distorted images of what human being looks like. If we do catch a glimpse of forgiveness in the looking glass it is more likely than not to be some unflattering image such as "forgive and forget," or the notion that forgiveness means condoning bad behavior (letting people "get away with something" they shouldn't), or the thoughtless reflection that forgiveness and reconciliation always go hand in hand. Sometimes the reflection we see in the mirror is not only distorted but frightening: "I don't get mad," a popular bumper sticker reads, "I get even." The false mirrors of our world routinely bombard us with likenesses that tell us revenge is sweet and forgiveness is just too damn hard for us mere mortals and better left up to the divine.

"Now we see in a mirror, dimly . . ." Paul wrote in his first letter to the church in Corinth (1 Cor 13:12, NRSV). When we wake to the carnival games that all earthly mirrors play, we can also come to realize that the true reflection of forgiveness in our world is never to be found in any mirror of glass and silver, but simply in each other's eyes. "The only true voyage of discovery . . ." Proust wrote, is "not to visit strange lands but . . . to behold the universe through the eyes of another, of a hundred others, to behold the hundred universes that each of them beholds, that each of them is; and [then] fly from star to star."[2] Now *that's* a mirror worth consulting. And just as we see more when we look with our heart, we see forgiveness reflected more clearly in each other's eyes when we keep our heart polished and free from the dust and streaks and fingerprints that life leaves all over it.

There is, in fact, a scientific basis for this kind of reflective mirror in the heart, and it unfolds not in our chest but in the in-between places firing data all day long in the dark cranial cave where our brain resides. I am certainly no neuroscientist, but I take the word of those who are and say that their research into just how our noggins work has revealed specialized collections of cells in our brains called "mirror neurons."[3] These mirror neurons not only assist us in learning new skills by observing others engaged in the same task, but also in language development and even self-awareness, feelings like empathy, and how we relate to and understand each other.

In a very real way we are mirrors of forgiveness. We find forgiveness neuron by neuron, reflected eye to eye, and heart to heart.

2. Proust, *Remembrance of Things Past*, 657.
3. The implications of this discovery are explored more fully in Iacoboni, *Mirroring People*.

DAY FOURTEEN

Next Time Won't You Sing With Me?

> They said to each another, "What is it?" For they did not know what it was.
>
> —EXOD 16:15

> As soon as we start putting our thoughts into words and sentences everything gets distorted, language is just no damn good.[1]
>
> —MARCEL DUCHAMP

HERE IS ANOTHER STORY from the desert fathers. Abba Arsenius was having a conversation with an elderly Egyptian monk, asking him many questions. Overhearing this conversation, another brother commented, "Abba Arsenius, you have a strong education in Latin and Greek. Why do you discuss anything with this peasant?" He replied, "True. I have knowledge of Latin and Greek, but I do not yet know this man's alphabet."[2] How beautiful, and humbling, to think that we each have our own alphabet yet still might learn each other's language; that we are incarnate

---

1. In Shlain, *The Alphabet Versus the Goddess*, 393.
2. Bangley, *By Way of the Desert*, 179.

letters ready to be put together into whole and holy sentences and paragraphs. Forgiveness too has its own alphabet—its own grammar and syntax—and is, if ever there was one, an incarnate word. It was never intended to be a fixed entry in the musty pages of some old dictionary, but rather meant to be lived out and felt and embodied.

But, we humans naturally name and define things; it's what we do. The trouble is that forgiveness, like some other languages, appears to employ an alphabet that has no vowels—or at least not vowels that we readily recognize—where some or all vowels are assumed and not necessarily written out. And so we're left to fill in the spaces between the consonants for ourselves, like the rabbinic fathers or the ancient scribes of so many Semitic languages. Such languages rely more on word roots that are composed mainly of consonants instead of syllables with various prefixes and suffixes. In Arabic, for example, the letters *k*, *t*, and *b* combine to form a root that connotes something like "to write." Fill in the spaces in-between and from this *ktb* root we get the related words for "he wrote" (*kataba*), "writer" (*kātib*), or even "book" (*kitāb*). It seems awkward and cryptic at first but even eyes and brains accustomed to English can look at the letters *f-r-g-v-n-s-s* and easily factor in the necessary o's and i's and e's to manifest forgiveness. If not, just ask your text-speak fluent teenager!

Since ancient Hebrew did not use any vowel markings, even the name of God is unutterable, ineffable, and ultimately unknowable. This is reflected in the most frequent designation for God in the Tanakh: *YHVH* (or transliterated into our Roman alphabet, YHWH), a combination of the four Hebrew letters *Yod*, *Hey*, *Vav*, and *Hey*. The letters are thought to derive from the three-letter root from which we also get the Hebrew verb "to be" (*hayah*). The name of God is therefore thought to be something like "That Which Is," although some scholars would go beyond that imperfect tense and offer "Is-Was-Will Be" as a more accurate translation for God's name.[3] To be or not to be, exactly how to pronounce

---

3. See, for example, Green, *These Are the Words: A Vocabulary of Jewish Spiritual Life*.

that sacred name remains unknown even after careful scholarship. This is partly because even the consonants we have to work with aren't much in the way of consonants, as they are more breath sounds than anything else. Tradition holds that when YHVH appears in sacred text it is not to be vocalized, but another word, such as *Adonai* ("my Lord") or simply *Hashem* (the Name) substituted in its place. Indeed, uttering the name of God was considered blasphemous and therefore it was only written and never spoken. Many Jews afford this same respect to the English translation of the Hebrew equivalent by writing it out as "G_d," intentionally leaving out the vowel.

We desperately want words to be defined and contained, to stay the same. And so we press them like precious petals between the leaves of heavy thick books. But in reality words are something so much more prismatic than that; they are "vehicles of hidden, deeper shades of thought . . . You can hold them up at different angles until light bursts through in an unexpected color."[4] These lines are very much in line with the rabbinic tradition, where it is said that every word of sacred Scripture has seventy faces and six hundred thousand meanings. Any interpreter knows that language both reveals and obscures, and understands the challenge is to seek out the word behind the word and go beyond the letter to the meaning hidden within.

We read, some of us, the New Testament in English. And every time forgiveness appears in that sacred text it appears as the same word: forgiveness. But in its more original language, forgiveness' appearances in the Bible are much more nuanced. Sometimes it is the Greek word *apolyō*, for example, meaning something like to set free or release. Sometimes forgiveness is more akin to *aphiēmi*, as in to send away. Still other times it is *charizomai*, or to show a kind of favor or kindness that cancels, in turn from *charis*, which can mean that most beautiful word—grace. Similarly, in the Hebrew Bible more than one word is used to refer to forgiveness. Hebrew even allows for the nuanced difference between the forgiveness practiced amongst humankind and that forgiveness

---

4. Morrow, *The Names of Things*, 4.

which only *Hashem* can extend to us. To put it in plain English, over time and through translation after translation we have come to define forgiveness so much more narrowly than the space it holds open to us.

When we explore the alphabet of forgiveness we see that the word is seemingly interconnected with a whole family of other words: apology, confession, sin, contrition, absolution, pardon, punishment, mercy, and reconciliation among them. But while these associated words are related to the act of forgiveness they are not forgiveness itself, even if we may have been taught they were. Still, their prominence colors to what extent we are prepared to forgive. They remind us of how we learned about such a word as forgiveness in the first place and how we actually use it—or not—in our daily lives. The fact is we have substituted a whole host of words as surrogate terms for forgiveness in our vocabulary regardless of whether or not they are synonymous. At the same time we have forgotten the notion that, as in so many languages, there can be more than one kind of forgiveness and more than one way to say it. We've made the word all capital letters in our tongue, italicized it, underlined it, and surrounded it with quotation marks—exclamation point. In reality, it can emerge from our everyday alphabet, if we choose, as something less embellished, more humble. A plain and simple small-letter word: forgiveness.

Even in the quantifiable discipline of science there is a concept known as critical realism; we are not capable of knowing everything and therefore even scientific theories are subject to revision, translation, and change. In other words, scientific understanding and discovery are driven not only by the quest for truth and fact and knowledge, but also by a humble and holy curiosity. It is a concept related, in its very alphabet, to the escaping Israelites standing astounded in the desert knee-deep in life-giving manna, a gift from heaven. "What is it?" they asked. They hadn't a clue what it was, no name by which to refer to it, not enough letters in their alphabet to spell it out. And yet they still trusted it would sustain them day by day and bring them from where they were to where they longed to be.

DAY FIFTEEN

Turning the Page

Everything is held together with stories. That is all that is holding us together, stories and compassion.[1]

—BARRY LOPEZ

You write your life story by the choices you make.[2]

—HELEN MIRREN

IN THE BEGINNING WAS the story. This statement unfolds from a re-consideration of how the opening of the Johanine gospel—"In the beginning was the Word"— has been, or could also be, translated. Interestingly, the word that allows for such re-consideration is the word *word* itself, or more accurately *logos* in the gospel's original Greek. There really isn't a precise English equivalent for *logos*, but word works. However it's not the only possibility. Some translators would suggest *message* or *utterance*, for example, or even *wisdom* or *reason*. In Hebrew the word for "word" can also mean "think." Story, though—as in *the* story—feels somehow

---

1. In Evans, "Leaning into the Light," 62–79.
2. In Mirren, "Helen Mirren."

right, even if our ears have grown accustomed to hearing another: word.

From our very beginning we inherited an alphabet with which to construct and direct and redirect the story of our life. Of course we were not aware then of how our stories, those we tell about ourselves and those we tell to ourselves, might shape who we would become. We ourselves are chapters in the stories of those who brought us into the world and, for better or worse, raised us. At first our vocabulary was pretty simple and so was our story. But all good stories eventually lead to some plot twist or another and the story line gets complicated. The old words no longer adequately describe.

We write the stories of our life one sentence at a time. The challenge is to see each other as new words—as ever-emerging texts—and to read each other's sentences as if they were sacred. As we are. Paul said as much in his second letter to the Corinthians, that we are letters to be read and known, "written not with ink but with the Spirit of the living God, not on tablets of stone but on tablets of human hearts" (2 Cor 3:2–3). Sometimes, though, we need to be translated. Sometimes a chapter or verse gets misinterpreted. Sometimes the story is hard to read and we're tempted to close the book and walk away. But all every story ultimately asks of us is to turn the page. And yet, too often we get stuck on page one, on what happened then and there, and dwell there. Our memory tells us tales over and over, like a forgetful old relative who asks parenthetically, "Have I told you this before?" but then goes on with the all-too-familiar saga anyway. Similarly, we just as frequently sign off on someone else's version of our own story. We forfeit authorship each time we cast our own character as the victim. Listen carefully; I am not saying that we should deny reality—bad things happen. But once upon a time was only once upon a time. Just as critical to the story, if not more so, is how it ends.

And *we* get to write that part.

There will undoubtedly be times when it feels as if others are manipulating the plot twists of our life, when really they are writing their own story. We have been and will be hurt and disappointed in life. But let's be clear about what part of that narrative is about us and what part isn't. To look gently back and understand that sometimes the story is more about other people being incapable of giving us what we really needed—whether love or dignity or respect—or that they were simply doing the best they could, even if that wasn't good enough for us or we deserved better. Or, there may be times when we become our own scene-stealers and need to forgive our very self; moments when we face the most difficult task of extending self-forgiveness, while granting our self the mercy of reframing the story in a way that reflects not a singular action in time but our truest nature. Either way, the story is only ours to tell. But if we never turn the page, we never realize how everything turns out in the end—that something totally unexpected happens in the next chapter. Ultimately, our story has no beginning or end—only arbitrary moments from which we either choose to look back or look forward.

Staring at the blank page, we pick up our pencils and write. The scene is set; the characters are all in place. The question is what story will we tell today? Which story will we live into? Will we continue with some version of Descartes' classic exclamation—*cogito, ergo sum*—twisting it into "I was hurt, therefore I am," or "I will not love, therefor I am safe?" Or, can we somehow transcribe that existential statement into the holy sentence, "I am because we are,"[3] or even "I forgive, therefore I am wholly human?"

Or maybe the question is which end of the pencil should we be using? Will we continue keeping track of what's wrong, of past offences and hurts, or will we turn the pencil around and start erasing?

---

3. This is one translation of the wonderful African word and way known as "Ubuntu," which can also be translated as "a person is a person through other persons," or even that "what makes us human is each other." This concept was instrumental in an entire nation's quest to acknowledge, forgive, and move forward from a tragic moment in time, namely the so-called Truth and Reconciliation Commission hearings held in South Africa after the horrors of Apartheid. See Tutu, *No Future Without Forgiveness*, and Battle, *Ubuntu*.

DAY SIXTEEN

Tongues of Fire

Listen and understand. What goes into someone's mouth does not defile them, but what comes out of their mouth, that is what defiles them . . . the things that come out of a person's mouth come from the heart . . .

—MATT 15:10-11, 18

Watch your thoughts; they become words. Watch your words; they become actions. Watch your actions; they become habit. Watch your habits; they become character. Watch your character; it becomes your destiny.

—TAO TE CHING

THE DESERT MYSTICS HAD a saying: "If you desire a spiritual pilgrimage, begin by closing your mouth." Perhaps they were recalling the words of James in the Bible: that the tongue, though a small part of the body, can seemingly talk our whole being into trouble. "Consider what a great forest is set on fire by a small spark," James wrote, noting that "the tongue also is a fire" (Jas 3:5-6). It can steer the whole body in the wrong direction, setting the whole course of one's life ablaze. While our tongue and our temper are what usually get most of us into trouble, pride is what keeps us there. Or so the saying goes.

The Bahá'í faith teaches similarly that the tongue is a smoldering fire, that just as material fire consumes the body the fire of the tongue can devour both heart and soul. Both death and life are in the power of the tongue (Prov 18:21). The psalmist prayed for God to set a guard over his mouth and to keep watch over the door of his lips (Ps 141:3). And Paul reminded the church in Ephesus to "not let any unwholesome talk come out of your mouths, but only what is helpful for building others up according to their needs" (Eph 4:29). Even Gandhi had something to say about what comes out of our mouths, advising "In prayer it is better to have a heart without words than words without heart."[1]

Our words and our ability to utter and understand them are a defining characteristic of our humanness that sets us apart from all other species. The fact that we speak is one thing; how we speak to and about other human beings, however, reveals just exactly what kind of human we are. The Hebrew word for "word"—*davar*—is derived from a root that has to do with ordering thought, a reminder of the power of verbalization; that when we speak anything, we speak it into existence. In the beginning, God created the world by speaking its parts aloud: God said, "Let there be . . ." and it was so. The first book of the Hebrew Bible teaches that the entire world as we know it was created with those ten utterances (Gen 1).

James devoted nearly the entire third chapter of his epistle to the image of the tongue as wildfire and the challenge of governing such an incendiary device. Obviously our words matter enormously. Just as the smallest spark can ignite an entire forest fire, a tiny word spoken carelessly from our mouths can cause immeasurable harm. But the opposite is true as well: a heartfelt word of care or encouragement can inspire and bless its hearer and even remain with them the rest of their life. For good or ill, the words we use with each other have a life of their own. We learn as children that "sticks and stones may break my bones, but words can never hurt me." But everyone knows how absurd that silly old

1. In Kamath, *Gandhi*, 70.

nursery rhyme is. A bitter word spoken against us can continue to hurt much longer than the time it takes a broken bone to heal; it can become a more lasting injury, a festering wound. One line of Jewish thought compares negative speech to a kind of murder, a murder that kills not only the person to whom it is directed but also its speaker, along with anyone else who hears it as well.

But fire isn't only or always a force of destruction. We have always gathered around fire for warmth or food, and even the equally life-sustaining act of storytelling. Untamed, fire is dangerous; yet harness the energy within it and fire brings comfort and community and even safety. Writing of this potential energy, the French philosopher and Jesuit priest Pierre Teilhard de Chardin predicted:

> The day will come when, after harnessing the ether, the winds, the tides, gravitation, we shall harness for God the energies of love. And, on that day, for the second time in the history of the world, man will have discovered fire.[2]

While we may be getting closer and closer to that particular kind of fire, and forgiveness is growing warmer and warmer in our hearts, we may still find our tongues tied, unwilling to give it voice, to say the word forgiveness aloud. That's okay. Sometimes an important step along the way to forgiving is the intentional decision to no longer speak ill of our offender, to not even engage in the temptation to gossip or whisper about them behind their back. In other words, we can guard our tongue until it can wrap itself around the full syllables of forgiveness.

In the mean time we can rest assured that the word is in fact very near; it is on our lips and already kindled in our heart. We've only to fan into flame love's fire.

---

2. Teilhard de Chardin, *Toward the Future*, 86–87.

The Way of the Knowing Heart

DAY SEVENTEEN

The Heart of the Matter

Like one who takes away a garment on a cold day, or like vinegar poured on a wound, is one who sings songs to a heavy heart.

—PROV 25:20

Somewhere, far down, there was an itch in his heart, but he made it a point not to scratch it. He was afraid of what might come leaking out.[1]

—MARKUS ZUSAK

THE HEART IS A powerful muscle. We depend upon its steady beat to pump oxygen-rich blood to every living cell of our bodies. On average, the human heart beats 100,000 times every day of our entire life. As long as all is well we hardly give this loyal and tireless organ a passing thought, yet without it we could not survive. We understand, and take for granted, that the heart is a vital part of a vast and intricate biological system of blood vessels, arteries, veins, capillaries, blood cells, and plasma that in turn cooperates with other life-sustaining organs such as our lungs or kidneys or brains. And when it comes to healing wounds, we depend on the

---

1. Zusak, *The Book Thief*, 60.

heart to pump sticky platelets and other clotting agents as well as infection-fighting white blood cells to the sight of the injury.

We may think our hearts are just for circulation, but we've long seen them as organs of thought as well. We say we know a certain song or poem "by heart," for example, and no matter the matter before us we strive to get down to its "heart" in order to truly understand it. In many Asian languages the same word is used to mean both *heart* and *mind*. As one of the vital organs, the heart has a long history of being identified with not only life itself but also thought. The ancient Egyptians saw the heart as the seat of emotion, will, and intention. Many classical thinkers, including Aristotle—the man we still think of today as the father of science—disregarded the contributions of the brain in functions such as reasoning and intellect, and attributed those functions instead to the heart. With the development and advances of the disciplines of anatomy, physiology, cardiology, and neuroscience we most likely find such thinking absurd. Yet, something in that ancient thinking continues to ring true.

When we say "So-and-So has a good heart" we do not simply mean that person has a healthy ticker. What we're really trying to say is that person is caring, compassionate, empathetic, and means well in all things. We talk about a teaching reaching us at a "heart level" and we struggle to align "head and heart," phrases that suggest there are some things that can only be fully understood somewhere beyond the boundaries of our minds. Even the popular saying "don't just talk the talk, but walk the walk" is really about this alignment of thought and feeling, brain and heart. As vital as our hearts are to physical survival, perhaps they are even more essential to our spiritual growth. The word *heart* appears well over a thousand times in the Bible. The twelfth-century Christian mystic Hildegard of Bingen held that the soul lives in our heart as in a house. In sacred writings from many traditions the heart appears over and over as a symbol not just of our thoughts or feelings, but of our deepest selves, our spiritual core, and our very identity.

A relatively new field of medicine, neurocardiology, asserts that heart disease and the healing of the heart are not only about "the physical body but also the emotional, mental and spiritual bodies."[2] Research in this field finds that our heart and not our brain first processes our initial reactions to stressors; when the heart perceives a threat it tells the brain to send signals to produce stress hormones, which in turn leads to inflammation and further to the constriction of blood vessels, and elevated blood pressure.

Maybe Aristotle was on to something after all.

We can think about forgiveness all we want, study every doorway and threshold we step through, consider every possible path to venture down, look in every mirror, try on every possible sandal, shoe and boot, turn every page and explore every metaphor, but if our heart is not ready we won't get very far, if anywhere at all. The heart knows that healing takes time, wounds need careful attention, and even after healing the area surrounding the original hurt will probably remain tender for a period of time. Some wounds may even need to be reopened in order to drain and fully heal. Unlike the practical-minded heart, however, the head thinks up all kinds of crazy ideas about injury and hurt. Instead of circulating healing agents our brain too often circulates hurtful rumors; it avoids the issue, denies the fact that we may be in pain or, even worse, convinces us to drown our sorrows in alcohol or pop some pain-killing, mind-numbing pill. And then another.

But oh, when our heart is ready for a fresh beginning, there's no stopping it! In the land of forgiveness a good part of that readiness is a thorough assessment of the injury, to become as fully aware as possible of the depth and breadth of the hurt. Past hurts have real emotions attached to them and until we identify, acknowledge, and accept those feelings neither our head nor our heart will ever be ready for forgiveness. In order to continue with our day to day lives, we may have minimized or compartmentalized a hurtful event. Our heads can even half-convince us that there actually isn't any pain or lingering resentment at all. But by not bearing witness to the breadth and depth of a past hurt we also doubt the validity of our feelings, allow our brains to override our heart's truth.

2. Samuels, "The Brain–Heart Connection," 77–84.

The Way of the Knowing Heart

As we journey toward forgiveness our duty is to keep our head and heart attuned not only to the full nature of any past hurt, but also to make room for "good things to run wild"[3] in our hearts and minds, and to be open to unforeseen paths.

Today we remember what the Little Prince said on his wilderness journey: "you have to look with the heart."[4]

---

3. I borrow this phrase from G. K. Chesterton, who wrote, "The more I considered Christianity the more I found that while it had established a rule and order, the chief aim of that order was to give room for good things to run wild." See Chesterton, *Orthodoxy*, 95.

4. Saint- Exupéry, *The Little Prince*, 71.

DAY EIGHTEEN

Stone vs. Flesh

A new heart I will give you, and a new spirit I will put within you; and I will remove from your body the heart of stone and give you a heart of flesh.

—EZEK 36:26 (NRSV)

The chemist who can extract from his heart's elements compassion, respect, longing, patience, regret, surprise, and forgiveness and compound them into one can create that atom which is called love.[1]

—KAHLIL GIBRAN

AT THE VERY HEART of the Torah, which in turn we might think of as the heart of the Hebrew Bible, there is a statement that represents the heart of both Jewish and Christian, and maybe even all religious practice and belief: that we should love God—by whatever name—with all our heart, and with all our soul, and with all our strength. There is a wonderful story told by the rabbinic fathers about that familiar line from Torah and the one that immediately follows it; that we should lay those words upon our hearts (Deut 6:6). One curious student was particularly struck by

1. Gibran, *The Kahlil Gibran Reader*, 44.

the word "*upon*" in that line and consulted a wise rabbi about it. "Why doesn't the book tell us to put these words *in* our hearts?" he wondered. The rabbi answered, "That is because, as we are, our hearts have become hardened and the words cannot get in. So we lay them upon our hearts where they stay until something or someone breaks the heart open. Then the words fall right in."

Many things can break our hearts open: hurt, sorrow, loss, betrayal, disappointment, and rejection all come easily to mind. But a scene of great beauty can pry open our hearts, too, as can an uncontainable joy, a tender moment of love, a quiet moment of wonder, or a simple unlooked-for look from someone who understands. It seems our hearts were made to be broken. With luck, none of us will make it through life without experiencing some kind of heartbreak. For when calloused hearts of stone become renewed hearts of flesh there is still something more than and after heartbreak. Without disappointment we would probably never learn about change or how to grow and be and do things differently. Without experiencing grief and sorrow ourselves we would never be able to be truly empathetic or compassionate, to have a heart that understands others.

What breaks our heart somehow heals it.

Abba Poemen said, "The nature of water is yielding, and that of stone is hard. Yet if you hang a bottle filled with water above the stone so that the water drips drop by drop, it will wear a hole in the stone. In the same way the word of God is tender, and our heart is hard. So when people hear the word of God frequently, their hearts are opened . . ."[2] Yet, the true life of our hearts is love. Without love our hearts grow heavy. Conversely, our hearts fill, flutter, pine for and race at its prospect. The twelfth-century Muslim mystic Ibn al-'Arabi wrote that, "When the heart embraces reality, it is as if reality fills the heart."[3]

Today we are offered the miraculous possibility of a heart transplant; the chance to swap out our old heart of stone for a new one of flesh—an open heart, a heart of compassion—even if the

---

2. Nomura, *Desert Wisdom*, 59.
3. Ibn al-'Arabi, *The Bezels of Wisdom*, 148.

mechanics of such a transformation are beyond our understanding. Our hearts can either reject that possibility or open up to embrace and be filled with the reality of forgiveness. The choice is ours. No matter our decision we might benefit from spending a moment with the old adage that says, "the person who does not make a choice, makes a choice." We do not arrive willy-nilly at forgiveness. We get there by deciding to go there. We choose to forgive. We also choose not to forgive. Stone or flesh, the heart beats on night and day whether we are aware of its steady rhythm or not. The heart is even awake as we sleep.

Today, imagine forgiveness dripping drop by drop over the heart-stone sitting in your chest.

Tonight, before going to sleep, choose to place the word forgiveness upon your heart with the sure confidence that it will someday fall in.

DAY NINETEEN

Forgive and Remember?

I will pass beyond this faculty of mine called memory; I will pass beyond it and continue resolutely toward you, O lovely Light.[1]

—ST. AUGUSTINE

Let us remember that there is a creative force in this universe . . . a power that is able to make a way out of no way and transform the dark yesterdays into bright tomorrows.[2]

—DR. MARTIN LUTHER KING JR.

ANY VENTURE INTO THE wilderness of the heart and mind requires that we also cross through the landscape of memory. Saint Augustine realized this as he was composing his *Confessions*, the extended and intimate prayer he wrote sometime in the fourth century yet still illuminates. "Now I arrive in the fields and vast mansions of memory," he wrote, where treasured and innumerable images are brought in by our senses. "There too are hidden away the modified images we produce," he added, "when by our thinking we magnify or diminish or in any way alter

---

1. Augustine, *The Confessions*, 286.
2. King, *A Call to Conscience*, 198.

the information our senses have reported."[3] For Augustine that landscape was more expansive than how most of us tend to view memory; it shared a border with the divine and the eternal and transcended time. But he pointed out right away the fickleness of our memories, how we modify, magnify and diminish them.

We tend to fossilize our memories and the past, or at least believe we can, compressing them until they seem to solidify even as time steadily marches on. We try to convince ourselves that those memory rocks are as solid as real fossils, that they are somehow proof. But in a fossil all that's really left behind is only the ghost of a skeleton, whether that of a leaf or some age-old creature—an imprint of what once was—with which we're left to wonder and hypothesize about what really existed. Memory is neither fixed nor static; not an unsuspecting fly stuck in amber and frozen in time, but something much more alive than that—a constantly metamorphosing creature.

Of all the misconceptions about forgiveness the ill-guided notion of "forgive and forget" is perhaps the most discouraging. It is one of our greatest obstacles to forgiving, for we are made to remember; our survival depends upon our ability to recall. There is a part of memory that preserves and protects; without it we would constantly put our finger into the flame to see if it burns. We forgive precisely because there is something that we do remember: a particular event or offense. Hurtful words or acts are not easily erased from our memory banks. Our brains are simply not wired that way, to wake up one morning and say and believe that a certain thing never happened. Yet we've so adopted that all-too-familiar saying—forgive and forget—into our culture that we spend day after day, year after year worrying about the fact that since we cannot forget we must therefore not be able to forgive . . . until in our mind the saying becomes the ultimatum: "forgive *or* forget." Or at the very least "I can forgive but I cannot forget," which when it comes right down to it is really no different from saying, "I cannot forgive."

None of which is really true.

3. Augustine, *The Confessions*, 273.

Yet even the Bible tells us that God will forgive and forget. Speaking through a prophet, God says, "I will forgive their wickedness and will remember their sins no more" (Jer 31:34). But surely that divine amnesia is not the same kind of forgetfulness as when we forget where we left our keys, or cannot remember someone's name. Just as there are so many ways to remember, there must be different forms of forgetting.

Ultimately, there is no past tense to forgiveness: "Memory is more than a looking back to a time that is no longer, it is a looking out into another kind of time altogether where everything that ever was continues not just to be, but to grow and change with the life that is in it still."[4] Forgiving requires remembering and never asks us to forget. It simply asks us to deny anger, hurt, and resentment the opportunity to take over our lives. Forgiveness does not deny that something happened; it denies that the event has the power to control our present and our future. It is not the erasure of the past but a letting go of a desire for the past to be different from the way it was.

Today we ditch this unhelpful phrase once and for all. The Prophet Muhammad offered another option: "pardon and overlook, until Allah delivers His command" (*The Qur'an*, al-Baqarah 2:109). The eighth-century Jewish prophet Isaiah offered another alternative: "Do not dwell on the past—See, I am doing a new thing!" (Isa 43:18–19). Forgive and not dwell . . . a notion that suggests we neither permanently erase the memory of an offense, nor abide within it; but choose instead to go on with life while not allowing the memory to dictate and dominate our life.

The Rev. Michael Lapsley, a South African Anglican priest offers still another choice. As a chaplain to students in both black and white universities in Durban, South Africa, in the 1970s he witnessed the horrors of apartheid firsthand, and spoke out on behalf of those who were being shot, detained, and tortured. In 1976 (the same year as the Soweto Uprising) he was expelled from the country and lived in the mountain kingdom of Lesotho, where he became a member of and chaplain to the African National

---

4. Buechner, *The Sacred Journey*, 21.

Forgive and Remember?

Congress in exile. After a police raid in 1982, in which forty-two people were killed, he moved to Zimbabwe, where he was sent a letter bomb by a covert operation of the apartheid security forces. He lost both hands in that explosion, along with the sight in one eye, and was seriously burnt. He does not preach "forgive and forget," but rather, "Heal and Remember" through a series of workshops offered by his subsequently founded Institute for the Healing of Memories.

Barbara Kingsolver concluded her wonderful novel, *The Poisonwood Bible*, with one of the story's characters telling her guilt- and resentment-riddled mother, "Slide the weight from your shoulders and move forward. You are afraid you might forget, but you never will. You will forgive and remember."[5]

We do not forgive and forget. We forgive and do not dwell; we heal and remember. We forgive as we remember; we remember to forgive. Today we remember there is something very important that we should not forget. We make a note to ourselves and stick it on the refrigerator, we tie a string around our finger, we program our clock or watch or phone to "beep" us a reminder, or we ask a friend to remind us in person that we seek every day not the forfeit of forgetting, but the grace of remembering . . . forgiveness.

---

5. Kingsolver, *The Poisonwood Bible*, 543.

DAY TWENTY

It Has a Song, It Has a Sting, Ah, Too, It Has a Wing

Gracious words are a honeycomb, sweet to the soul and healing to the bones.

—PROV 16:24

Last night while I was sleeping I dreamed—blessed illusion—I had a beehive in my heart, and from my old bitterness the gold bees were contriving white combs and sweet honey.[1]

—ANTONIO MACHADO

THERE IS BOTH SWEETNESS and a sting to memory. While forgiveness does not ask us to forget, our remembering is not necessarily always pleasant. Still, as Archbishop Desmond Tutu reminded, "It is important to remember . . . Forgiveness does not mean condoning what has been done. It means taking what happened seriously [and] drawing out the sting in the memory . . ."[2] Perhaps the novelist Sue Monk Kidd had it right, when she

---

1. Machado, *Border of a Dream*, 87.
2. In Ford, *The Sacred Art*, 74.

It Has a Song, It Has a Sting, Ah, Too, It Has a Wing

reminded her readers that we should not be afraid of stings in life; bees sting us as a last resort and to do so means death for the little insect. Yet, neither should we be unprepared. Standing in the bee-yard of forgiveness we would do well to remember to don long sleeves, and not swat:

> Don't even think about swatting. If you feel angry, whistle. Anger agitates while whistling melts a bee's temper. Act like you know what you're doing, even if you don't. Above all, send the bees love. Every little thing wants to be loved.[3]

We sing at the break of every New Year, so many of us, that old Scottish tune: "Auld Lang Syne." Indeed, the song is sung at many endings and beginnings throughout the year, probably because it asks that tender question, "is it better to remember the past or not?" To look backward or forward? Of course the product of that age-old question depends on what we choose to remember. We can repeatedly regurgitate past hurts and carry a grudge, which is as Charles Gerber pointed out, "like being stung to death by one bee," or we can engage the song's new year, new day, new moment question with longing and hope, an emotion the great agnostic Robert Ingersoll asserted was "the only bee that makes honey without flowers."[4]

Honey has long been considered a symbol of wisdom and purity, poured as a blessing over foundation stones of temples or offered to God as a symbol of sweetness. An entire chapter of the Qur'an is named after the honeybee: surah an-Naḥl. During Rosh Hashanah, or the Jewish New Year, one of the traditional foods eaten on that day is apple slices dipped in honey to embody and foretell of the sweet days to come. Early Christians were given a cup not of wine, but of milk and honey after their baptism as a symbolic welcome to the elusive Promised Land alluded to in the Hebrew Bible. Bees have always flickered and fluttered in our imaginations.

---

3. Kidd, *The Secret Life of Bees*, 92.
4. Gerber, *Healing for a Bitter Heart*, 74; Baker, *An Intimate View*, 91.

The Way of the Knowing Heart

Desmond Tutu's observation that we can remember and at the same time "draw out the sting of memory" comes from his experience of leading his country through what had been a far from sweet history of brutal discrimination and violence—apartheid—toward a more hope-filled future. The Archbishop was called to chair a new court-like restorative justice body, which would become known as the Truth and Reconciliation Commission (TRC), and whose mandate was "to bear witness to, record and in some cases grant amnesty to the perpetrators of crimes relating to human rights violations." Far from forgetting the past or saying, "Let bygones be bygones," the TRC delved deeply into the stinging stories of those on all sides of apartheid. There was no automatic amnesty for perpetrators because it was felt that such a blanket amnesty would be akin to something like a national amnesia. The process was never about forgetting the whole thing ever happened, but the power of witness and the possibility of amnesty in exchange for truth and taking responsibility. In many cases, such truth-telling also led to both public and private acts of forgiveness.

In her most influential work, the political theorist Hannah Arendt observed that while we have the faculty to remember the past we are powerless to change it, a persistent challenge in our human existence. She concluded that the only effective response to this challenge was forgiveness. The great Irish poet, William Butler Yeats, hoped to find himself someday on Innisfree, an iconic island of his imagination, where he would build a cabin and grow rows of beans and tend to a hive of honey bees, and live alone there in that "bee-loud glade." The Belle of Amherst was referring to fame when she penned the words that serve as title to today's meditation, but they fittingly describe our focus as well: the past—our memory—has a song. So too it has a sting.[5]

And it can take wing.

The humming life of the hive is a collective one, though. Bees, not unlike us, are highly social creatures; the success of the colony depends upon a kind of hive-mind, on how well each individual gets along with all the other members of the community. Today we

---

5. Dickinson, *Complete Poems*, 713.

It Has a Song, It Has a Sting, Ah, Too, It Has a Wing

practice the sweet bee-attitude of remembering in order to heal, of bearing the sting of memory in order to arrive at the sweet nectar of healing.

Blessed are those who remember, for they will move beyond bitterness.

DAY TWENTY-ONE

Mind Over Matter
—or—
Saint Paul Was a Neuroscientist

Do not conform to the pattern of this world, but be transformed by the renewing of your mind.

—ROM 12:2

The mind is its own place, and in itself, can make a Heaven out of Hell, a Hell of Heaven.[1]

—JOHN MILTON

IT TURNS OUT YOU *can* teach an old dog new tricks. In direct opposition to the long-held belief that once we've done something a certain way for so long learning how to do it differently is well-nigh impossible, science has proven otherwise. Neuroscientific research indicates that our thoughts, behavior and experiences can actually reshape and redirect our neural pathways and synapses, or how our brains organize information, as well as—remarkably—the actual structure of our brain itself. As recently as

---

1. Milton, *Paradise Lost*, 279.

the twentieth century, brain research held that our noodles were relatively cooked after a critical period, namely childhood, and the structure of our brains remained pretty much unchanged the rest of our lives. More recent findings reveal that many aspects of the brain remain trainable and flexible even well into adulthood.

As groundbreaking as this research is, awareness of the ability of the mind to change the brain to transform the mind is nothing new. Saint Paul's directive, "Do not be conformed to this world, but be transformed by the renewing of your minds," can easily be recognized today as an exercise in neuroplasticity. We will never quite fully know what happened on Paul's life-altering journey to Damascus, except that this man was not on his way to praise Christ or his followers, but to persecute them. The man that encourages us to rewire our mind was intimately familiar with that process—he was the same man who, in his youth, ordered an early disciple of Jesus to be stoned to death. That we can completely turn our minds around was no ordinary assignment in imagination for Saint Paul.

"The greatest discovery of my generation," said the late nineteenth-century psychologist, William James, "is that a human being can alter his life by altering his attitudes of mind."[2] No matter if our gray matter is used to thinking of forgiveness as unattainable or even in a certain, peculiar way. Our minds can physically rewire our brains, not only by how we think but by how we choose to be with each other, a kind of inter-relational neuroplasticity, if you will. Sri Ramakrishna, a Bengali mystic that significantly shaped the development of modern Hinduism, espoused that meditating on an ideal was a sure way to acquire its nature. This is the bedrock of the journey we are on: thinking about forgiveness for forty days and nights, we hope to acquire the nature of forgiveness. To do that we must be willing to constantly sit on the edge of our life and unlearn everything that may have helped guide us in the past but is no longer helpful in the direction we are now headed.

Change of heart, change of mind . . . neither one comes easily or quickly. Like insects transforming from egg to larvae to pupae

2. In Ruggiero, *Making Your Mind Matter*, 26.

to full-winged adults we change in increments. But each stage along the way is truly transformative; what hatches from the egg looks nothing like what emerges from the cell of honeycomb, the chrysalis, or the cocoon.

The Greek word most often translated to repentance in the New Testament is *metanoia*. But the meaning of that original Greek word is very different from what twenty-first-century English-listening ears are accustomed to hearing. There is none of the sorrow, contrition, or regret we usually associate with repentance in its original language, which was first translated (or, more rightly, mistranslated) into the Latin phrase *paenitentiam agite*— "to do penance"—before being translated again into the English word we recognize: repentance. We've come to think "repent" as it appears in the New Testament means "to be sorry." But originally it had a whole lot more to do with changing the way our brain works; about radically changing the way we see the world in order to change the world around us for the better. For in biblical Greek, *metanoia* signifies a complete change of mind, heart and life, a mighty and magnificent change in what we think, what we do, and how we live.

Even Tertullian, who has been called the father of Latin Christianity and the founder of Western theology, argued that *metanoia* in its original Greek, is not so much about our confession of sins as it is about radically changing our ways and mind. While we use our minds in reading scripture, we must also allow those holy words to descend into our hearts in order to gain their full impact. If we all read the Hebrew Bible, the New Testament, the Qur'an, the Upanishads—or any sacred scripture, for that matter—with our minds only we would have long ago dismissed them as absurd. We discover and discern holy words not in encyclopedias and dictionaries, but in our hearts and minds.

And forgiveness is one of the holiest of words.

We may, in fact, recognize in that Greek word for change of mind the prefix, *meta*, from the word we associate with caterpillars somehow morphing into winged butterflies: *metamorphosis*. Changing our thoughts is nothing to scoff at; it is the most radical kind of work. For in renewing our mind, to use St. Paul's words, we not only turn, but re-turn to some primal location; we change not only our minds, but also our hearts and, indeed, our very cellular make-up. We become no longer conformed to a world of inching along on our bellies, but transformed into denizens of a world of flight and air and space.

Nothing stays the same; everything changes.

We grow wings.

DAY TWENTY-TWO

The New Math
Practice Makes Perfect

Then Peter came to Jesus and asked, "Lord, how many times shall I forgive my brother or sister who sins against me? Up to seven times?" Jesus answered, "I tell you, not seven times, but seventy-seven times."

—MATT 18:21–22A

Practices are not for know-it-alls. Practices are for those who feel the need for change, growth, development, learning. Practices are for disciples.[1]

—BRIAN MCLAREN

IN ALGEBRAIC EQUATIONS AN unknown number is often represented by some letter of the alphabet. Such ciphers can be identified through logic and calculation: figure out the value of "y" and "z" and the meaning of "x" comes clearly into focus. Countless children learn this every day in school. For me, algebra was a subject I tried desperately to understand but couldn't quite grasp. My parents struggled along with me trying to help. But they had

---

1. McLaren, *Finding Our Way Again*, 137.

THE NEW MATH

never studied algebra in their one-room schoolhouse and found it equally confusing. They called it, not entirely optimistically, "the new math." Too much talk of square roots and they'd be off on some other tangent, more often than not about tubers—their school stories were always rooted in skiing or sledding to school with baked potatoes in their pockets to keep them warm. Recalling those kitchen-table homework memories from my adolescence, as well as our current journey, I cannot help but think too of C. S. Lewis who, writing about forgiveness, noted that, "When you start mathematics you do not begin with the calculus; you begin with simple addition."[2]

But then, we come to Jesus's answer to Peter's question in the Matthean gospel. What are we to make of this odd number: seventy-seven times? (Indeed, some translations have it as "seventy times seven" times.) Is this just more of the Wild One's crazy math? After all, wasn't he the one who multiplied five barley loaves and a couple of fishes into more than enough to feed five thousand? Or taught that the first shall be last and the last shall be first? Maybe Jesus' algebraic answer to Peter's question, "How often should I forgive?" should come as no surprise to us after all—Jesus multiplies.

We should keep in mind, though, the time and place of Peter's question. He was not living in present-day wherever. The one who is considered today as the rock and foundation of the early church was not yet even a Christian as we understand the term; Christianity had not yet evolved. Rather, Peter most likely would have been familiar with the teachings of the Hebrew tradition, which says that you should ask another for forgiveness up to three times.[3] Poor Peter, he probably thought he was being generous with his offer of "as many as seven times." Yet Jesus still managed to

---

2. Lewis, *Mere Christianity*, 116.

3. A tradition upheld by the book of Amos, where God pronounced judgment on the enemies of Israel with the words: "For three transgressions of Damascus, and for four I will not revoke its punishment" (1:3). In that same chapter God pronounced similar judgments against several other nations, always with the words, "for three transgressions . . . and for four" (cf. vv. 6, 9, 11, 13) In other words, each of those hostile nations was permitted three offenses that God overlooked, with the fourth offense being a different consideration.

significantly expand his arithmetic, offering Peter—and us—a new kind of math: "Not seven times, but, I tell you, seventy times seven times." By the standards of Peter's world that calculation made no sense.

By the standards of our world it still makes no sense; we would prefer that forgiveness have a limit. But Jesus was not merely outlining some mathematical equation. What Jesus was really saying was that Peter—and each of us—ought to forgive as long as we live. The number seven is invoked throughout Scripture as a symbol of perfection or completion. And when we look around for the number seventy we need not look any further than the book of Psalms (90:10), where the length of our human lives is estimated to be "threescore and ten," or seventy years. Jesus was not suggesting that we literally multiply forgiveness seventy by seven times, and then on the four-hundred-and-ninety-first time withhold forgiveness, but that forgiveness is more of an ongoing process, a way of being that lasts for the length of our entire lives.

This notion is echoed in the Gospel of Luke as well, where Jesus says, "If your brother or sister sins against you, rebuke them; and if they repent, forgive them. Even if they sin against you seven times in a day and seven times come back to you saying 'I repent,' you must forgive them" (17:3–4). Again, Jesus turns forgiveness from a "one and done" action to an *ad infinitum* aspect of being alive, a lifelong way of being with each other.

"We are what we repeatedly do," Aristotle famously said. He also said that we learn the things we have to learn before we can do them exactly by doing them. His observations hold true for any number of qualities or characteristics, including forgiveness. We know from our earliest experiences—from learning how to walk to how to ride a bike—that if we want to excel in something we must engage in it repeatedly with attention and determination in order to improve our facility and skill. If we practice resentment, we will get better at resenting; if we practice forgiveness, we will become more adept at forgiving. The modern dancer and choreographer Martha Graham understood the importance of practice when she wrote wisely:

The New Math

"Whether it means to learn to dance by practicing dancing or to learn to live by practicing living, the principles are the same. In each, it is the performance of a dedicated precise set of acts, physical or intellectual, from which comes shape of achievement, a sense of one's being, a satisfaction of spirit. One becomes, in some area, an athlete of God.[4]

Today, as disciples of forgiveness, we *practice* forgiveness.

---

4. In an essay written for the NPR radio program, "This I Believe," aired circa 1953, and subsequently published in Carter, *The Routledge Dance Studies Reader*, 66.

The Way of the Desert Stream

DAY TWENTY-THREE

The Desert Shall Rejoice and Blossom

The land that you are crossing over to occupy is a land of hills and valleys, watered by rain from the sky.

—DEUT 11:11 (NRSV)

As the rain and the snow come down from heaven, and do not return to it without watering the earth and making it bud and flourish, so that it yields seed for the sower and bread for the eater, so is my word that goes out from my mouth: it will not return to me empty, but it will accomplish that which I desire and achieve the purpose for which I sent it.

—ISA 55:10-11

RAIN WASHES AND REFRESHES; our survival depends upon its merciful replenishment. We can go without food for some time if we have to, but without water our time quickly comes to an end. Without rain we thirst. Rain sustains our bodies as well as our planet. Replenishing and generous, rain is also humble; once it falls from above its shape becomes no longer a drop but something else: a puddle or stream, a sprouted seed or stalk of wheat, a child in bright yellow galoshes or a green frog glistening in the

The Way of the Desert Stream

grass. It is, as Saint Teresa of Ávila proposed, impossible to divide or separate the water belonging to a river from that which fell from the heavens.

Rain falls all over the Hebrew Bible and the New Testament. The notion of physical thirst as a metaphor for spiritual need—and God's constant promise to provide, to quench, to pour out—flows right through their pages. The title of today's meditation reflects one such promise (Isa 35:1), but the prophet's pages are sprinkled throughout with quenching invitations: "Come, all you who are thirsty, come to the waters" (Isa 55:1). The Psalmist's soul pants for God "as the deer pants for streams of water" (Ps 42:1). In the wilderness the Israelites grew grumpy with thirst and grumbled at Moses, "Why did you bring us up out of Egypt to make us and our children and livestock die of thirst?" (Exod 17:3). Moses struck a rock, at God's command and promise, and the people had drink abundant. Not to rain on our parade, but there is also that part where it rained cats and dogs, pitchforks and hammer handles, for forty days and forty nights, after which God made another promise to Noah and to us: the rainbow set in the clouds (Gen 9:12-13).

In the New Testament the rainbow makes another appearance, this time as a symbol of a future covenant between God and all people in the book of Revelation (4:3). Much in the same way, throughout the New Testament everyone is looking for water that will eternally slake their thirst: "whoever drinks the water I give them will never thirst," Jesus says more than once.[1] Matthew reminds us in his gospel that salvation depends on sharing this water not only with each other, but more importantly, even to those whom we do not know well: "I was thirsty and you gave me something to drink . . ." (Matt 25:35–40). There is a physical form of liquid water in the Bible, so often in the shape of rain, that is necessary for survival, and a living water—not unlike forgiveness—that is just as necessary for life.

Both rain and the rainbow are fitting images to consider along our wilderness journey. We are thirsty for forgiveness and

---

1. A notion illustrated throughout John (4:13–15; 7:37–38; 19:38), and also Revelation (7:16–19; 21:6; 22:1, 17).

forgiveness quenches. Just as rain falls in the form of drops, so too does forgiveness; we feel a drop or two today . . . and a few more tomorrow, and before we know it forgiveness becomes a mighty river flowing from our heart. In this way, even the slightest drops of forgiveness can wear away even the most stubborn stone. The words we say to each other not only fall from our lips; they have a life of their own: "like the rain," the Sufi poet Rumi reminds us, "they will fall and spread, and their mystery will grow green over the world."[2]

A rainbow bends light and turns it inside out, offering us another view of something we have become accustomed to "seeing" a certain way. Invisible light, what once was colorless, explodes into a whole spectrum of tints, hues, shades, and gradations. Forgiveness, right as rain, does for our heart what the rainbow does for light, helping us to see reality no longer in black and white but in full color. Just as inside light there is a rainbow of colors, inside forgiveness there is a multitude of refractions of what life can look like.

The land that we are crossing over to on our wilderness journey is a land of hills and valleys, watered by rain from the sky. Today's weather forecast: forgiveness showers, rain or shine.

Leave your umbrella behind. Soak up every drop.

---

2. In Harvey, *The Way of Passion*, 2.

DAY TWENTY-FOUR

A River Runs Through It

> All streams run to the sea, but the sea is not full; to the place where the streams flow, there they continue to flow.
>
> —ECCL 1:7 (NRSV)

> The river delights to lift us free, if only we dare to let go. Our true work is this voyage, this adventure.[1]
>
> —RICHARD BACH

EVENTUALLY, AS NORMAN MACLEAN wrote in his short story (with which today's meditation shares the same title) "all things merge into one, and a river runs through it."[2] Out of Eden flowed a primordial river that separated into four others—the Pison, the Gihon, the Tigris, and the Euphrates—which, in turn, flowed to the four corners of the earth (Gen 2). Rivers flow throughout the Hebrew Bible and into the New Testament, which ends with an angel presenting yet another river, one that flows by the throne of God and by which Eden will be restored (Rev 22:1), circling

---

1. Bach, *Illusions*, 17.
2. Maclean, *A River Runs Through It*, 104.

back again to those original waters of Genesis. That river was immortalized in the old hymn, "Shall We Gather at the River."

Rivers are inseparable from many religions. The river is holy in Hinduism; in fact that religion has seven holy rivers and many others whose waters are significant. A dip in any one of those waters is thought to cleanse one of sin, an act that reverberates with the splash and dunk of Christian baptism, first performed also in the river, as we know from the story of Saint John the Baptist. Just as our stream of consciousness is seldom logical or linear, and no river's course is perfectly straight and narrow, the river of forgiveness twists and turns, and delights in the surprise of those revolutions. The river has a way of singing in many voices, of sliding into other ways of being and taking us along with it, something more than a few writers have recognized. It's difficult to imagine, for example, Huck Finn—indeed even the author of his adventures—without the mighty Mississippi, or the *Wind in the Willows* without its River Bank.

When we come to the banks of a river we arrive at the very shores of our life. The trek to forgiveness may seem some days like a scorched and arid place with no oasis in sight. But God makes not only a way in the wilderness for us to follow; God also provides us the welcome sight of a river in the desert (Isa 43:19). And should we need to get to the other side God will be with us in that crossing: "When you pass through the waters, I will be with you; and when you pass through the rivers, they will not sweep over you" (Isa 43:2), a line that is surely meant to recall yet another water crossing, the parting of the Red Sea, from whose banks the Israelites began their own exodus through the wilderness. According to the Apocrypha, when the Israelites were in that wilderness, thirsty and confronted only with waters from a bitter stream, God put a tree into those waters to make them sweet, even though the Israelites were complaining and grumbling once again (2 Esdras 1:22–23). The biblical Jacob wrestled with a mysterious being on the banks of another waterway, the river Jabbok, the night before he would be reconciled with his twin brother Esau with whom he had been fighting, we are told, since they were still in their mother's womb

The Way of the Desert Stream

(Gen 32:22–32). Like Jacob, perhaps we too have something we must wrestle with on our own journey to forgiveness—old ideas, underlying assumptions, unhelpful thoughts—along the banks of the River Life.

Still wet from his baptism in the river Jordan, Jesus went immediately into the wilderness where he faced his own doubts and demons. It isn't beyond reason to imagine that Jesus asked those flowing waters to carry away whatever was too heavy or burdensome for him, what he could not conceive of carrying with him into his own journey in the wilderness. So too we are invited to set down on the banks of today's river what we need not carry any further.

There is a wonderful word of encouragement spoken amongst pilgrims on the Camino de Santiago, the Way of Saint James, the ancient pilgrimage trail established in the ninth century which leads to the Spanish shrine to that saint at Santiago de Compostela. The rallying cry, "*Ultreya!*" used by pilgrims to greet and encourage along the way, is a medieval Spanish word meaning "Onward!" with the exclamation point being an additional note of encouragement and perseverance. A more contemporary translation might be "to the end" or even "go for it!" The river is, perhaps, the ultimate pilgrim; whether traveling surreptitiously underground or overflowing its banks, its only mission is to carry its headwaters to their very destination. No matter if there is no direct route. Rivers delight in meandering and enjoy every twist and turn, gaining strength from each adjoining tributary and cascading waterfall along the way. Neither do they hurry, for they know that there is nothing more likely to reach its destination than a river wending its way surely home to the fathomless sea.

Ultreya!

DAY TWENTY-FIVE

The Water Bears No Scars
Stumbling Blocks vs. Stepping Stones

Therefore let us stop passing judgment on one another. Instead, make up your mind not to put any stumbling block or obstacle in the way of a brother or sister.

—ROM 14:13

Only the strong current, eddying in deep mid-channel and flowing like a long and hastening ripple past the banks, carries a hint of what is presently to come.[1]

—HENRY BESTON

WHEN A RIVER COMES across something that might potentially block its progress it merely finds another way, flowing around or under or over and past the obstruction. Rivers are accepting by nature; they yield to the shape of whatever landscape they happen to be traveling through, whether gully, ridge, or hollow. Even so, the river does not cease its patient glide and flow toward its ultimate destination: some as yet unseen sea. Neither does

---

1. Beston, "The St. Lawrence," 67.

the river stop to brood over any bumps or scrapes inflicted by impediments in its path. Indeed, though water yields, all things must ultimately yield to the river. Even granite boulders in its path are eventually worn away by its constant movement.

In the book of Psalms, rocks are a recurring sanctuary: "For in the day of trouble [God] will keep me safe . . . and set me high upon a rock" (27:5); "[God] set my feet on a rock and gave me a firm place to stand" (40:2). In fact, rocks in the river can even be helpful; they trouble the water, pointing out the current and how swiftly the river runs its course. We may wish for peaceful shores in life, for lazy rivers and tranquil pools shaded and overhung by sheltering trees, but—counterintuitively—life is most lavish where waters are the most disturbed. All kinds of things inhabit the in-between elemental space where liquid water meets seemingly solid surface and mixes with air. What we can reckon from rapids, from the intersection of rocks and rivers, is that where water is the most ruffled it is the richest in oxygen, a basic building block of life as we know it. Turbulence is not terrible, but teaches.

A popular spiritual from the turn of the last century put it well: "we've got to wade in the water, child, 'cause God's gonna trouble the water." The song references stories from both the Hebrew Bible and the New Testament. The verses are yet another reference to the parting of the Red Sea and the Israelites' escape into the wilderness. The chorus echoes the story of "The Healing at the Pool" related in the fifth chapter of the Gospel according to John, where it is said that an angel stirred from time to time the waters of a certain pool that was near the Sheep Gate in Jerusalem, and known in Aramaic as *Bethsaida*. Whosoever stepped first into those troubled waters would be healed. To that place a number of people in search of healing made pilgrimage. One who had been an invalid for thirty-eight years, we are told, was constantly trying to be the first to step into those "troubled" waters to be healed. But, since he had no one to help him in, someone else was always the first. "Then Jesus said to him, 'Get up! Pick up your mat and walk.' At once the man was cured; he picked up his mat and walked" (John 5:8–9).

When it comes to forgiveness we don't need to walk on water. We can hop from one ancient stone to another until we've forded the river and reached the opposite bank. Whether the river is an actual course of water or an image of life flowing by, the trick is to recognize the rocks as stepping stones rather than constantly stubbing our toes on them like stumbling blocks. To listen to what rocks in the river have to teach us.

We've already bumped into a few stumbling blocks on our journey so far: the dead-end of required apology, the complicating maze of "forgive and forget," and the trap doors of expectations and assumptions, just to name a few. But chances are there will be plenty more rocks in the river: breached trust, needing to be right, the notion that some people just don't deserve forgiveness, and the insidious way that we can actually become comfortable with our loneliness, resentment, and anger. We would rather not admit to the fact, but there's even a river rock that has our own pettiness written all over it. In truth, there's a self-righteous judgmental part in all of us—let's call it ego—that simply doesn't even *want* to forgive others in the first place and derives some false sense of power, if not wicked joy, in withholding forgiveness.

The key is to become aware of, and acknowledge the rocks in our river and step over them instead of tripping on them over and over again. Sure, we might get splashed. Some stones might even be slippery. But probably the worst thing that might happen to us is a soggy sneaker. For that matter, we could simply take off our shoes, roll up our pant legs, and wade thankfully and barefoot into the troubled waters of forgiveness.

What stumbling blocks to forgiveness have you put in your own way in the past?

How might you turn those stumbling blocks into stepping stones?

DAY TWENTY-SIX

All Is Well

What makes the desert beautiful . . . is that it hides a well somewhere.[1]
—ANTOINE DE SAINT-EXUPÉRY

Some nights stay up till dawn, as the moon sometimes does for the Sun. Be a full bucket pulled up the dark way of a well, then lifted out into the light.[2]

—JALAL AL-DIN RUMI

IN THE WONDERFUL STORY *The Little Prince*, one of the things that both the title character and the narrator (a stranded pilot) search for, along with love and friendship, is water. They are wandering through a desert, after all. When they finally come to a well it is an extravagant affair, not a simple hole dug deep into the desert sands, but one that looked as if it could sustain an entire village, except there was no village in sight. Yet everything was prepared and waiting for them: the deep pool of clear water, a

---

1. Saint Exupéry, *The Little Prince*, 68.
2. In Barks, *The Essential Rumi*, 279.

rope and pulley, and an attached bucket with which to draw up the sought after.

The well is a metaphor for all that is deep. Sometimes that depth is the waters of clear thinking. Other times it is the stagnant, muddy waters of our bitterness and pain. An old farm adage goes like this: "What's down in the well comes up in the bucket." As any good well is deep we need a way to extract the desired liquid and so we make use of the rope and pulley and bucket. But the bucket pulls up only what is in our wells to begin with. In addition, we would benefit from inspecting the condition of the assisting devices before we employ them. The desert mystic Evagrius Ponticus said, "If you harbor grievances and offenses and yet think you are praying, you are doing nothing more than drawing water from a well and pouring it into a bucket that is full of holes."[3]

There are any number of ways a well can be compromised and contaminated. If we've polluted our inner well with anger and resentment, for example, we should not be surprised to pull up an overflowing bucket of bitter water. We too easily fill our wells to overflowing with hatred, with envy, with vengeful thoughts. Living in the middle of the desert of unforgiveness, we walk every day to the well of victimhood, the well of withdrawal and self-distancing, the well of self-righteousness . . . the well of, well—fill in the blank.

Kabir, the mystic poet and saint of India, wrote tellingly that what we search most desperately for is all around us: "Look at you . . . screaming you are thirsty / And are dying in a desert / When all around you there is nothing but water!"[4] Similarly, when it comes to the waters we seek, the Igbo people of Nigeria believe that forgiveness is present all around us; all we need to do is reach out and pull it into our being, take a long cool drink of its refreshing waters.

Through our thoughts and actions and words, we can choose to tap into this most potable and dependable aquifer, the quenching waters of forgiveness. "A good man brings good things out of the good stored up in his heart, and an evil man brings evil things

---

3. Bangley, *By Way of the Desert*, 372.
4. In Harvey, *The Direct Path*, 36.

The Way of the Desert Stream

out of the evil stored up in his heart," Jesus is recorded as saying in the gospels, "For the mouth speaks what the heart is full of" (Luke 6:45).

There's no guarantee that once we arrive at the well of forgiveness that everything will be in working order. The rope may have frayed in the desert sun. If we have not made use of it for so long, the pulley may be stiff and rusty. Indeed, when the Little Prince and the pilot first began to draw water from their well its rusty pulley squealed and groaned. Undeterred, the prince said to his new friend, "Hear that? We've awakened this well and it is singing."[5] So too, we might have to awaken our own well of forgiveness in order to hear its song.

Further still, we must be willing to dip our buckets into the deep, unfathomable waters of forgiveness in the first place; to take the risk of lowering ourselves into the deep dark chamber that is the way of any well, as Rumi wrote so tenderly, in order to be, "lifted out into the light."

We may thirst for forgiveness, but forgiveness is so much more than merely a quenching drink. Our friends from *The Little Prince* understood well what was really in the well. The pilot, worried over the effort it took for his frail and failing friend to pull up the bucket of water, helped hoist the full bucket to the edge of the well: "I am thirsty for that water," said the Little Prince. "Let me drink some . . ." Then, in a moment of tenderness, our narrator understood what they had been looking for all along, and that it was a gift meant to be shared. He raised the bucket to his friend's lips and the Little Prince drank. It was water and quenching, but it was more than that:

> It was as sweet as a feast . . . It was born of [their] walk beneath the stars, of the song of the pulley . . . It did the heart good, like a present.[6]

We might be a little rusty when it comes to forgiveness, but today we awaken the well of its waters and listen for the gift of their

---

5. Saint-Exupéry, *The Little Prince*, 69.
6. Ibid, 71.

All Is Well

song. Still, we have all we need: the rope, the pulley, the bucket, and the deep well of forgiveness.

DAY TWENTY-SEVEN

Setting Sail

Crossing the Unknown Sea of Forgiveness

Look at ships: though they are so large that it takes strong winds to drive them, yet they are guided by a very small rudder wherever the will of the pilot directs.

—JAS 3:4 (NRSV)

The winds of grace blow all the time. All we need to do is set our sails.[1]

—SRI RAMAKRISHNA

MORE THAN TWO THIRDS of our planet's surface is salt water. Like the river, the sea also beckons. We've long been fascinated by its recurrent rhythms of surge and surf and swell, its constant ebb and flow, its sheer breadth and depth, and by its soothing tranquility as well as its unpredictable and mighty power. Without the awesome sea we would not have "Amazing Grace," surely one of the world's most recognized hymns. Its author, John Newton, grew up the son of a commander of a merchant ship and joined his father at sea early in his childhood. Later in life he became

---

1. In Chang, *Wisdom for the Soul*, 530.

captain of his own ship, one enlisted in the slave trade. During one such voyage his ship came into a violent storm and when all seemed lost he turned to prayer. Ultimately saved, Newman came to believe that God had spoken to him through the tempest and that a saving grace had begun to unfold in him. He went on to become a clergyman as well as an outspoken voice in the campaign to abolish slavery.

The ocean has been the literary setting for so many life lessons, from Homer's *Odyssey* to Hemingway's *Old Man and the Sea* to that epic story of revenge, Herman Melville's *Moby Dick*. The ocean has always inspired; its rhythmic tides echoing our human breath, the crest and trough of each one of its waves a reminder of the possibility of movement and change.

Yet even today the sea is not completely known. Its depths remain, in many ways, unfathomable. We might even think of it as the last great frontier of our planet. In other words, the ocean is yet another wilderness, albeit a watery one. Forgiveness can often feel like a mighty ocean, a vast dimension where wind and wave and currents and tidal forces all combine to act and pull against or for us. Sometimes it appears we are simply adrift. Other times we may feel like we are lost on some remote latitude of regret, resentment, or remorse. Still other times, we drop anchor and refuse to sail any further.

In Melville's leviathan tale of unforgiveness, the protagonist Captain Ahab becomes increasingly lost at sea, even though he knows the ocean like the back of his hand. Adrift and awash in the deep waters of revenge, Ahab loses all sense of bearing and in his quest for vengeance imperils not only his own life but the entire crew of his ship, the *Pequod*, a fictitious nineteenth-century whaling ship out of Nantucket. Along his savage sea voyage, Ahab meets Boomer, the captain of yet another whaleship, the *Samuel Enderby* of London. Like Ahab, he too has lost a limb to Moby Dick, one of his arms, but rather than harbor any ill-will toward the mighty whale Boomer councils Ahab to forgive and leave the whale alone. But of course, Ahab chooses otherwise. As the story ends, the captain of the *Pequod* is granted the opportunity to exact revenge upon his nemesis. The harpoon is lifted, and then launched. But as Ahab throws the spear into the great white whale, he becomes entangled in the ropes and riggings—we might even say the tangle of revenge itself—and is pulled into the sea where he drowns.

In order to arrive at the shores of forgiveness, we must become mariners attuned not only to the sea's tides and currents but also to which winds are blowing and whether to sail with or against them. The winds of vengeance steer our ship in one direction only, and it is not the way we want to go. We may need to lower our sails or change the angle they face in order to catch a more conducive current of air. We need the wind to propel us across the ocean, but our movement and voyage also depends upon a steady hand at the rudder. Saint James reminds us that even the largest of ships are guided by something as small as a rudder, and even the smallest alteration in its position can radically redirect a wayward ship. Our words—or as James would say, our tongues—are like rudders that steer the vessel of our life, but so too are our thoughts. How we speak about and to others and how we think about forgiveness influence what harbor we end up in.

More often than not, however, we never even set sail to begin with, but remain anchored in port, moored to the pier of fear. We look out to the sea's farthest edge and imagine, like our ancestors from generations past, not the possibility of something else lying beyond the horizon, but a frightful place where ships drop off the edge of our flat world. We get stuck there in the doldrums, where no wind blows, believing that maybe someday we'll even catch a glimpse of the ghost ship *Apology* on the horizon and sailing our way. Or we toss overboard the anchor of "why should I be the one to take the first step?" and settle in below deck.

But if we are learning anything on our journey it is that forgiveness is not an event so much as it is a way; not a safe harbor but a voyage, a movement from one place to another. Forgiveness is not one dimensional, but has breadth and depth and height and dimensions beyond those of this physical world, this world we know isn't flat. The key is to bravely set sail, to pull up our anchor, to circumnavigate our unknown sea, like Magellan and Sir Francis Drake and countless others did before us. To have faith in the force of buoyancy, the pull of tides, and the guidance of the heavens above as we steer our ship safely home.

"Traveler, there is no road; only a ship's wake in the sea."[2]

---

2. Machado, *There Is No Road*, 55.

DAY TWENTY-EIGHT

The Opposite Shore

They came to the other side of the sea . . .

—MARK 5:1 (NRSV)

And then it seemed to him that as in his dream . . . the grey rain-curtain turned all to silver glass and was rolled back, and he beheld white shores and beyond them a far green country under a swift sunrise.[1]

—J. R. R. TOLKIEN

A CORE PRINCIPLE IN the tradition of Mahāyāna Buddhism is the concept of *bodhichitta*, or the intention to bring all sentient beings to enlightenment. Its path includes the practice of the Six Perfections, or *Pāramitās*: being generous and compassionate, morally aware, tolerant and patient, diligent and determined, practicing mindfulness at all times, and always seeking wisdom. *Pāramitā* is an ancient word, Sanskrit in origin, which is often translated as "arriving on the other shore." Buddhism teaches that the world in which we live is a place of troubles and the source of those troubles is the tripartite waters of earthly desire, karma,

---

1. Tolkien, *The Return of the King*, 310.

and suffering. Enlightenment, not unlike forgiveness, awaits seekers on the opposite shore of those waters. The Six Perfections are often likened to rafts or small boats that help ferry us across from the world of suffering to the elusive "far green country"—to use Tolkien's fine words—on the other shore. We may lose sight of land in between those two shores. But then, what mariner ever discovered someplace new without first losing sight of wherever they had come from?

Still, we're apt to find the prospect of losing sight of the shore more than a bit intimidating: to set out from all we've ever known in order to arrive at what we hope for. But perhaps what the writer was trying to say is that the setting out is just as important as the arrival, and that beyond each day's horizon is the constant presence of possibility. Just as Augustine asserted that to seek God is to have found God, Buddhism's Six Pāramitās are not only like life boats, a means to an end, they are also the ideal itself. For by practicing being compassionate, tolerant, mindful, aware, and wise we are always arriving at another, better shore. In other words, the crossing is the arrival; the voyage is the destination, the opposite shore.

Painters would have us think otherwise, but there is sometimes a moment far out at sea and before one's final destination can even be perceived, when light and atmosphere combine just so that it can appear there is no horizon at all—where the sky and the sea seemingly fuse into one seamless element. Just as deceptive is how the horizon seldom seems to come any closer; that it is not a stationary location but something that travels along with us, always just ahead. How we arrive at forgiveness has much to do with how we frame it. And frame it we do, desperately trying to paint it a certain way and nail it to one place, hang it in a museum, catalogue it as a precious artifact, or tack a brass plaque beneath it that tells what century it's from.

But forgiveness cannot be so easily contained; its horizons go on and on, like an ever-expanding circle, like the rings and ripples that radiate out from raindrops as they make contact with the still surface of water. We cannot fully comprehend forgiveness unless we take a 360-degree view. In the bigger picture, forgiveness requires that we fully inhabit the center of the life we already have and take a good look around—all the way around.

Perspective and understanding are not immutable; we are quite capable of expanding our horizons. Just as at one time we thought the earth was flat, so too we used to think the universe was finite and revolved around us. Then, a new astronomy revealed a sun-centered, infinite universe expanding ever outward. Round is right; the primordial shape is the sphere, from atom to globe to the very core of our universe. In the beginning the earth was formless. Eventually it took on a shape: God created something round (Gen 1:2). And God now sits enthroned above that sphere (or circle, or globe, or round ball, depending on which translation of the Bible you consult) that we call Earth (Isa 40:22). The very gift of vision itself, of how we perceive the round world in the first place, depends upon our spherical eyeballs. Why not, then, consider forgiveness also as an infinite sphere? The metaphor is an ancient one. Classical Greek thinkers, medieval Christian mystics, mathematicians, scientists, philosophers, and astronomers have all employed the image of the infinite sphere to describe everything from nature to the universe to the Divine—and so we apply it to that which we seek to understand: Forgiveness is an infinite sphere whose center is everywhere and whose circumference is nowhere.

The way to forgiveness is not flat; there is no edge or end from which we will fall off. Only a new horizon always just ahead and boundless vistas opening ever outwards.

The Way of the Fruitful Field

DAY TWENTY-NINE

Groundwork
Cultivating Forgiveness

Break up your fallow ground . . .

—HOS 10:12 (NRSV)

If anything is certain, it is that every one of life's trials, if only because it breaks the hard crust of our physical and mental habits, creates, like the ploughing of a field, an empty space where seed can be sown.[1]

—PAUL TOURNIER

ACCORDING TO THE BIBLE the first earthling was fashioned out of the earth itself, a notion expressed by the word *adam*, from *adamah*, meaning "ground." In the beginning, we are told, God formed the first human from the dust of the ground, and reminds us that we shall eat bread until we return to it, for out of the earth we were taken (Gen 2:7; 3:19). We are dust, and to dust we shall return, an idea underscored in the liturgy for Yom Kippur: "Dust am I in my life; even more so in my death." The psalmist reminds us that God "knows how we are formed; [and] remembers that

---

1. Tournier, *Creative Suffering*, 138.

we are dust" (103:14). In my tradition, the oft-quoted words "earth to earth, ashes to ashes, dust to dust" are often said at the burial of someone who has died—a nod to these and other Biblical references. Our dusty beginnings are also related in the Qur'an (al-Ḥajj 22:5).

We are inescapably connected to the ground we walk on, the source of our most divine origins. Perhaps that explains the custom in so many religious groups of removing one's shoes or other foot covering before entering places of worship or any sacred space. It was quite common in the ancient world, for example, for worshippers to remove their sandals when entering the temple. Some historians would suggest that this action had to do with not tracking in dirt from the outside world, an idea that all of us have probably been reminded of more than a few times, having been children once, the evidence of our outdoor recreation all over our boots or sneakers threatening the recently mopped or otherwise cleaned floors of our childhood home. But that certainly was not the case with Moses when he stood barefoot before God who spoke to him from within a burning bush on Mount Horeb. God explained, "Take off your sandals, for the place where you are standing is holy ground" (Exod 3:5). The Muslim tradition of removing one's shoes before entering a mosque is rooted in this same story: "Indeed, I am your Lord, so remove your sandals. Indeed, you are in the sacred valley" (*The Qur'an*, ṬāHā 20:12).

Like Moses, we find ourselves on holy ground in the wilderness. And, like Moses, we take off our shoes not only in reverence to that holy ground, but in order to come closer to it, to be more intimate with it; to let it make contact with our skin—the soles of our feet as well as our very souls. Feeling that sacred earth beneath us, we are invited to plant a few more seeds of forgiveness there as well. Many years after Moses, Archbishop Desmond Tutu recalled moments during the Truth and Reconciliation Commission hearings in post-apartheid South Africa when forgiveness was so present and palpable, when offenders' apologies for horrendous crimes and their pleas to be received back into the community were met with confounding applause, that he whispered, "Let's keep quiet, because we are in the presence of something holy . . . Really, we ought to take off our shoes, because we are standing on holy ground."[2]

Jesus and his disciples lived and taught in an agrarian society, communities where life depended on the very ground, on the planting and tending and harvesting of food crops, and their lessons often reflected the day-to-day reality of that farming life. In all three Synoptic Gospels one can read several such agricultural allegories: parables of mustard seeds, of picking grain on the Sabbath, of weeds growing amidst the wheat, or of the sower sowing seed. But the overall theme is planted throughout the Synoptic Gospels as well as the gnostic Gospel of Thomas. The original hearers of these parables would have deeply understood their intended metaphors because they understood both the greatest challenge and ultimate secret of any wilderness: if you cultivate it, it can become a fruitful field. In a very real way, Jesus taught that our lives themselves are like fields to be planted, tended, and harvested—that every particle of our lives, every patch of earth upon which we tread, every square inch of every one of our days is holy ground. What matters is whether or not we realize it: "Earth's crammed with heaven, and every common bush afire with God," wrote the poet Elizabeth Barrett Browning, "But only he who sees, takes off his shoes."[3]

Still, it would be folly no matter how blessed the soil may be to stick the stems of flowers, whether forget-me-nots or the blossoms of forgiveness, into the ground and expect them to flourish. Florence Nightingale, the foundress of modern nursing warned about just such a temptation in a letter to her nursing students: "There is a great temptation . . . to be in a hurry—to scratch the ground and not dig deep: to do surface work: like sticking in cut flowers, instead of sowing flowers and fruit too from the seed or

---

2. See Tutu, *No Future Without Forgiveness*, 151; Tutu interviewed in Hopkins, *The Art of Peace*, 101; and Brudholm and Cushman, *The Religious in Response*, 142.

3. In O'Grady and Wilkins, *Great Spirits*, 45.

root."[4] Likewise, we can neither harvest forgiveness in full bloom until we've planted the tiny seed from which it sprouts, nor plant that seed until we've dug deep and carefully prepared the soil for its roots to take hold.

Whether you use a hand shovel, rototiller, ox-drawn plow, or tractor, turning over the upper layer of soil brings long buried nutrients to the surface and, at the same time, buries both weeds and other green material, allowing them to become nutrients to be overturned and put to use in the future. This kind of cultivation helps create a rich and fertile layer of topsoil that encourages healthy growth. As we journey toward forgiveness, we can plough under what may have prevented successful germination in previous planting seasons and open up a more welcoming space in the holy ground of our lives. We can make straight furrows and plant acre after acre of forgiveness.

Jesus said, "No one who puts a hand to the plough and looks back is fit for service in the kingdom of God" (Luke 9:62). It's a statement anyone who's ever tried to hoe a straight row for the beans, or stood behind a bucking tiller or team of draft animals with minds of their own, or even sat behind the steering wheel of a puttering tractor bouncing over the field can understand. It's tempting to look back and see how you're doing, but you'll never make a straight furrow if you do and things will get all out of whack. It's better to glue your eyes on a point in front of you—like the furthest fencepost in the field or the peak of the neighbor's barn in the distance or, in our case, forgiveness itself—and never let your eyes stray from that spot. If we're serious about the journey we're on we must keep our eyes trained on where we want to go.

In his first letter to the Corinthians, Paul wrote, "Whoever ploughs should plough in hope" (9:10, NRSV). Abba Antony said: "Having therefore made a beginning, and set out already on the way to virtue, let us press forward to what lies ahead."[5]

---

4. In Dossey et al., *Florence Nightingale Today*, xviii.
5. Keller, *Oasis of Wisdom*, 70.

DAY THIRTY

The Sower Sows the Word

Be patient, therefore, beloved . . . The farmer waits for the precious crop from the earth, being patient with it until it receives the early and the late rains.

—JAS 5:7 (NRSV)

Just as there are seeds in the soil, so too there are secrets in the soil. The right seed touching the right secret can produce an abundance of new life.[1]

—MACRINA WEIDERKEHR

ON SEED STARTING DAY it seems incredulous that the small, seemingly lifeless specks sprinkled over the soil are capable of producing the trailing, tumbling, or towering plants that will grow and set fruit later in the season. Personally, were it not for the fact that each year in the garden I have seen with my own eyes the miraculous evolution of seed into plant, I wonder if I would even believe in the possibility of such complete transformation. That every seed contains everything required for a full-grown plant and some secret knowledge of what that plant will be; how

1. Wiederkehr, *Abide*, xvii.

many leaves it will have, how thin or thick its stem will be, how many branches, the tint and hue of its flowers, its height, and what fruit it will bear. If I consider the orchard beyond the garden, that there can be an entire tree hidden inside a miniscule seed—well, I cannot help but wonder about the utterly unbelievable. Further still, beyond even the orchard, there are wild apple trees that were planted, probably unawares by some deer or bear or bird, and grew by some unknown, enduring force. Their bountiful branches now miraculously stretch out over old dirt roads, hedgerows, and back-woods meadows alike. All this from a tiny little seed, a seed in which there was hidden a God-sized dream—a dream we may not fully grasp or be able to prove yet still can believe in. Or as an old Welsh proverb puts it: "A seed hidden in the heart of an apple is an orchard invisible."

Similarly, we can plant a thought or word—like forgiveness—in the orchards and gardens of our hearts. As in the botanical seed, we already carry within us the germ of all that we hope for, another God-sized dream. From the very beginning the endeavor of every seed is toward its fullest end. Jesus said, "The kingdom of God is as if someone would scatter seed on the ground, and would sleep and rise night and day, and the seed would sprout and grow, he does not know how" (Mark 4:26, NRSV). Sure, we may be able to explain germination on a cellular level. We can study and learn the required conditions that seeds need in order to thrive all we want. But, anyone who has ever expectantly dropped a seed into the dirt knows in their heart that every one of the physical requirements for germination—warmth, water, light, and time—revolves around the ultimate requirement of faith.

The question then becomes, what sort of fruit will we bear? And whenever will it be that we finally bear that fruit? What seed we plant influences the produce we will harvest. We reap what we sow. Plant a rutabaga, get a rutabaga. Neither do we expect to pick grapes from thornbushes, or figs from thistles (Matt 7:16). Our thoughts and actions have consequences. Just as the seed of resentment grows into anger; there are other seeds that will grow into forgiveness, seeds like awareness and intention, but also generosity, humility, and compassion. Patience and diligence often yield forgiveness as well. Here's another: giving people the benefit of the doubt. What are the seeds of forgiveness lying dormant in your life? What is preventing them from sprouting?

The parable of the sower and the seed, from which the title of today's meditation is taken, is found in the gospels of Matthew, Mark, and Luke. In it, Jesus tells the story of an apparently exuberant farmer who went out to sow his seed, casting them this way and that:

> ... some fell along the path; it was trampled on, and the birds ate it up. Some fell on rocky ground, and when it came up, the plants withered because they had no moisture. Other seed fell among thorns, which grew up with it and choked the plants. Still other seed fell on good soil. It came up and yielded a crop, a hundred times more than was sown (Luke 8:5b–8).

While there may be a particular lesson in this parable about how and where to plant, the wild abandon with which the farmer cast out the seed seems especially striking. That action could be seen as being oblivious or thoughtless, but there is also a certain hopefulness and trust to it that applies to the garden we are planting in the wilderness—to trust in both the seed and the soil, knowing that forgiveness will surely find a place where it will yield a hundredfold, or more. That's not to say we should haphazardly hurl the seeds of forgiveness hither and yon, and then forget all about them. We always need to cultivate the holy ground of our life. There'll be watering to do, and plenty of weeding too. Anger, for example, is an inherently human emotion and sometimes the appropriate response in the moment. But let it linger and it becomes a tenacious weed, putting down deep taproots and wrapping itself around every aspect of our being, until it becomes an in-grown hatred. The dandelion of disappointment, too, can spread if we're not careful, maturing into a barren of bitterness. The author of the epistle to the Hebrews warned, "See to it that no one fails to obtain the grace of God; that no root of bitterness springs up and causes trouble, and through it many become defiled" (12:15).

The Way of the Fruitful Field

The seed of forgiveness is already planted in you and me. Perhaps it is deeply buried or dormant, but it is there, just waiting to be unearthed and watered so that it might burst into life. We may sleep and rise night and day, but that seed will sprout and grow, though we know not how. Forgiveness is growing within each and every one of us, like an orchard invisible! Our task isn't to understand how such a thing could be possible. Our task is to believe in and tend to that seed; to cultivate it, water it, and keep the weeds from growing up around it.

DAY THIRTY-ONE

From Single Seed to Bountiful Harvest
Bearing the Fruit of Forgiveness

Very truly I tell you, unless a kernel of wheat falls to the ground and dies, it remains only a single seed. But if it dies, it produces many seeds.

—JOHN 12:24

Passing, passing / The blossom gives way to the fruit, / Both are necessary. / One passes into another.[1]

—JALAL AL-DIN RUMI

IN HIS FIRST LETTER to the church in Corinth, Paul wrote, "when you sow, you do not plant the body that will be, but just a seed, perhaps of wheat or of something else" (15:37). Inherent in that sowing is the idea that, while we reap what we sow, the mature plant we harvest looks very different than the seed from which it came. From the single kernel of wheat planted in the ground a stalk of new growth will rise, a stalk that will ultimately support a seed-head bearing up to fifty or more new kernels. Forgiveness

---

1. In Peck, *Bread, Body, Spirit*, 6.

is like wheat: a small kernel planted in holy ground. Given both darkness and light it will swell from the seed, erupting through the crust of our old patterns in order to bloom and set fruit, to multiply. But also inherent in this sowing is a certain sacrifice. For the seed that yields the fifty or more new grains gives itself completely to that transformation, surrendering its very identity and existence. The seed that gives new life dies in the ground.

Jesus spoke quite clearly about this: "Very truly I tell you, unless a kernel of wheat falls to the ground and dies, it remains only a single seed. But if it dies, it produces many seeds" (John 12:24). Seeds which, in turn, produce more seeds. Of course, Jesus was speaking metaphorically, just mere days before his execution, an end of which he was painfully aware. His reference to the kernel of wheat has long been interpreted to represent not only his own death and rebirth from the grave, but another kind of harvest: the hope and promise of a coming time of abundance. The truth is we are always dying in order to live. The cells that make up our being are constantly being sloughed off in order to make room for new ones. Scientists estimate that, in cellular terms, we are completely new entities every seven years or so.

And yet, there are stories upon stories of people holding on to a grudge for far longer, indeed, sometimes until the grave. As we sow forgiveness in our life, we must be willing to let the natural process of propagation occur; to let both life and death cycle back and forth in order to become something more. Our failure to let go of old patterns of behavior, of old ways of thinking like anger or resentment, or the need to be right, or our right to revenge is, perhaps, our greatest spiritual downfall. Instead of letting them fall into the dark, rich earth where they might arise into something new, we too often make our hurts immortal and let those malignant cells multiply instead, like a cancer that spreads, inhibiting healthy growth and ravaging the soul.

Each and every one of us struggles with our own hurts. I have mine, particular to my life, and you have yours, particular to your life. No matter the particulars, unless we let those hurts die we will never begin to truly live. But if we allow them to die, to fall into the dark, decaying compost of our former life, they will bear much fruit. They will swell and send out both sprout and root, and find the light as surely as the light seeks them. Of course, the choice is ours; we set down our old ways of our own accord. We have the authority to lay them down, and the authority to take them up again (John 10:17–18). Either way this death is not an end, but truly a beginning. And the law of nature reminds us that the returns always come multiplied. Old patterns of thinking are habitual and will come and go, like our breathing in and out. Our work is simply to be aware of their arrival and their departure; to let them come and go, to fall into the ground in order to birth something new.

The most miraculous aspect of forgiveness is that when we plant it in our hearts it can blossom not only there but in other hearts as well.

DAY THIRTY-TWO

The Wheat from the Chaff

As is the field, so is the seed; and as are the flowers, so are the colors; and as is the work, so is the product; and as is the farmer, so is the threshing floor.

—2 ESDRAS 9:17 (NRSV)

Beyond the entrance lay the place of separating the wheat from the chaff, or sorting and sifting, of beginning to cull that which would become bread.[1]

—JAN RICHARDSON

WE HAVE STEPPED THROUGH a number of thresholds on our journey to forgiveness and we will likely cross over still more. "To cross a threshold," wrote John O'Donohue, "is to leave behind the husk and arrive at the grain,"[2] a notion that nods to the origins of the word: the ancient entryway to the granary's threshing floor where kernels of wheat were separated from their stem and husk, where that which was of no value was stripped away from that which was prized. Nowadays, in the industrialized world we live

---

1. Richardson, *Night Visions*, 110.
2. O'Donohue, *To Bless the Space*, 193.

The Wheat from the Chaff

in, towering motorized combines that reap and thresh in one fell swoop take care of our amber fields of grain before they become bread. But in ancient times threshing and winnowing knew nothing of the variable-speed belt drives, hydraulics, or power take-off couplings of today's mechanization. Our forebears did it with their two hands and a liberal application of "elbow grease," sweat, and back-breaking labor.

Originally, the threshing was done entirely by hand, by beating the grains with a flail—two or more large sticks that were attached by a short chain—on the threshing floor of the granary in order to loosen the edible kernels. Later, another traditional method was to hitch donkeys or oxen to a central post and have them walk in circles or drive a cartwheel over the harvest on the hard surface of the threshing floor in order to free the sought after grains. Either way, until the invention of the first threshing machine in the 1700s, the task was laborious and time-consuming. After the threshing came the winnowing. This was done by tossing the resulting mash of grain and chaff, again by hand and using a basket, shovel, or a winnowing fork, into the air against the breeze. The dry husks and other parts would be blown away, while the more substantial grain would fall down to the ground to be gathered and stored. From this age-old process we get the old adage "separating the wheat from the chaff."

While the threshing floor was a practical, physical place, it didn't take long for it to acquire spiritual connotations as well and to be viewed as a place of blessing. Bible references to "the increase of the threshing floor" (Num 18:30, KJV), for example, and to a time when those "floors will be filled with grain" (Joel 2:24), spoke of more than actual grain, as did John the Baptist's prophetic words about Jesus: "His winnowing fork is in his hand, and he will clear his threshing floor, gathering his wheat into the barn and burning up the chaff with unquenchable fire" (Matt 3:12). Saint Paul continued the harvest theme in his first letter to the Church in Corinth (9:10). Similarly, winnowing took on equal symbolism: "You will winnow them, the wind will pick them up, and a gale will blow them away" (Isa 41:16), does not speak about mere husks and kernels of wheat. Neither does God's lamentation in Jeremiah: "I will winnow them with a winnowing fork at the city gates of the land" (Jer 15:7). All this is to say that for each of us there is both life-grain to harvest and accumulated chaff that needs to be swept away.

Yet chaff is an integral part of the plant; before it was removed from the grain it was simply known as the husk, a protective covering. Separating the wheat from the chaff is not necessarily so much about separating the good from the bad, but the useful from that which is no longer useful. Just as the kernel of wheat is enclosed within an outer husk, so too there are many concepts that closely surround forgiveness. To get at the kernel of what forgiveness is we may need to thresh away what forgiveness is not, to winnow away old assumptions in the breeze—assumptions like forgiving is the same thing as condoning or not holding others accountable for their actions. Forgiveness does not make what happened right or acceptable. It heals the hurt of what happened.

Another husk that closely surrounds forgiveness, and one we need to remove, is the notion that forgiveness and reconciliation go hand in hand. There are times when forgiveness may lead to reconciliation, and other times when, while it is healthy to forgive it simply would not be safe to reconcile. In addition, forgiveness in its most personal form requires only one person, the one doing the forgiving. Reconciliation is like the tango: it takes two. We can neither force another person to forgive or be forgiven, at least not authentically, nor require them to reconcile unless they, too, are ready. It is possible to forgive prior to, or even without the reestablishment of trust, but without restored trust reconciliation is wobbly, at best.

What is your wheat when it comes to forgiveness, its kernel of truth? And what has been your chaff?

The threshing floor holds one more lesson in forgiveness: to know when to stop threshing, when to let go. "Grain is crushed for bread, but one does not thresh it forever; one drives the cartwheel and horses over it, but one does not pulverize it" (Isa 28:28, NRSV). If you say "I forgive you," but continue to play the victim or martyr, you probably haven't let go. Nor will your words be believable. Where there is forgiveness, "sacrifice for sin is no longer necessary" (Heb 10:18). Or as Marlene Dietrich reportedly quipped, "Once a woman has forgiven her man, she must not reheat his sins for breakfast."

Today we leave our hurts and misunderstandings on the threshing floor just as they are, the wheat and the chaff, trusting that a sure and certain wind will take and sift them, retain for us what is worth keeping, and let the rest drift away.

DAY THIRTY-THREE

Allow to Rise

But if we hope for what we do not yet have, we wait for it patiently.
—ROM 8:25

The more patient and more open we are . . . so much the deeper and so much the more unswervingly does the new go into us, so much the better do we make it ours, so much the more will it be our destiny.[1]
—RAINER MARIA RILKE

"What are you waiting for? Do something!"

We've all heard those words hurled—if not at us, at someone nearby. The implication beneath and beyond the plea is that waiting is the same as doing nothing, or worse: a waste of one's time and equated with idleness and irrelevance; accomplishing nothing, killing time. Yet, the roots of the word *wait* reveal something quite the opposite. Originally the word meant something more akin to actively engaging in a certain watchfulness or keen attentiveness. Sadly, as is the fate of so many of our words, this rich meaning is all too often left out of the recipe that is our day-to-day communication.

1. Rilke, *Letters to a Young Poet*, 65.

Just as the image of the sower sowing seed and that image's corresponding themes of plowing, tending, harvesting, threshing, and winnowing grain wend their way through the Bible, so too does the theme of waiting. From the ancient Israelites who waited first in Egypt, then in the wilderness, and after that under Babylonian brutality, to the apostles whom Jesus told not to depart from Jerusalem, but to wait for God's promise, everyone in the Bible seems to be waiting for something, or someone. The Psalms are veritably expectant with waiting, and the author of Lamentations tells us that God is good to those who wait. Indeed, Noah waited for the floodwaters to recede; the recalcitrant Jonah bided his time in the belly of the whale; and in the twelfth chapter Lukan gospel we read that we should be like servants waiting for their master to come home from the wedding feast. But perhaps none of these embodies waiting more so than old Sarah, long expectant and finally pregnant with all she'd ever longed for, or Mary waiting with the Christ Child within. Or even the heartbroken father watching hopefully for the prodigal son's return. So too God watches patiently and attends always to our homecoming even as we, as the psalmist wrote, are weary from crying out and our eyes dim with waiting (Ps 69:3, NRSV) for that sure arrival.

Some things are worth waiting for.

Patience—with our self and with others, as well as patience with the process—is what makes forgiveness rise. That and the power of patience's two twin relatives: persistence and perseverance. Without their leavening all our efforts to knead our past hurts and present hopes into the bread we hunger for will fall flat; their addition makes all the difference in building the elastic structure that ultimately raises the accommodation we call forgiveness.

In the hands of the unhurried baker broken grain becomes bread. And yet time seems to be what we all are lacking; everything in our fast, faster, fastest-paced world seems to spin at the speed of light and still we can't keep up. No loafing around for us. Our breakfasts, lunches and dinners have all been fast-forwarded thanks to either the microwave oven or the drive-through lane. We've abandoned writing letters and talking on the phone, or—heaven forbid—face to face, for e-mail and instant messaging. If the notion of patience even crosses our minds, we pray that we might receive it immediately. Why not the same for forgiveness, too?

We run from patience, from diligence and determination, from dwelling in anything that may take time. We all too often seek—and expect—an on-demand dispensation at the press of a button; an instantaneous, quick fix, no waiting, express-line kind of forgiveness; a twelve-items-or-less, thank you very much, kind of forgiveness. (The irony is that while real forgiveness does take time, diligence, and patience, if we wait for it we can come to see that forgiveness, in fact, arrives in the blink of an eye.)

Leaven, in the Bible, symbolizes a kind of hidden transformation where what will eventually become the finished product—whether for good or naught—is set in motion. You don't necessarily see it working, and just a little bit goes a long way. "If the part of the dough offered as first fruits is holy, then the whole batch is holy," Paul wrote to the Romans (11:16). Conversely, when it comes to a believing community, he cautioned, just a little bit of sin can corrupt the whole lot (Gal 5:8–9). All three synoptic gospels caution against the permeating yeast-like nature of erroneous thinking. Yet once in Matthew (13:33) and once in Luke (13:20–21) Jesus positively equated our ultimate way of being to leaven: "The kingdom of heaven is like yeast that a woman took and mixed into . . . flour until it worked all through the dough." The comparison echoes the parables of the seed sown and tended and is yet another metaphor for growth—one of patience—where the hungered for arrives mysteriously and quietly.

While this description of heaven most likely would have shocked the original hearers of Jesus (predominantly Jews who celebrated Passover and reverently honored the memory of a slapdash, unleavened bread) the point is that the yeast itself is neither inherently good nor evil. It is merely an agent of multiplication: a once-dormant yeast cell thrives in the presence of warmth and food; the carbon dioxide released in the process is what leavens the loaf. What it multiplies depends on what you feed it. The real question is what kind of loaf do you want to end up with: a stale, hard brick full of dried up old resentments that catches in your throat; or a sweet rich challah, all golden and studded with sweet fruit?

While some of the elements of bread must first be put together in order for the process to begin, those elements require time to complete the transformation. After the yeasting a bread recipe will often advise the baker to "let the dough rest." This interlude allows both for the ingredients to meld, as well as for the gluten in the wheat or grain to relax, making for a stronger, more resilient and elastic network to form. So it is with our forgiving hearts. The word *rest* also has ancient roots that matter, ones that travel back to the Greek *hesychia*, a term that can also mean to pray and is at the very heart of the Orthodox contemplative tradition. Like dough, we ourselves are transformed through this kind of prayer/rest, brought that much closer to being the bread for which we hunger.

Today we allow ourselves to rest, ever watchful.

We wait . . .

We rise.

DAY THIRTY-FOUR

Bread of Heaven

I will rain down bread from heaven for you . . .

—EXOD 16:4

We are made of stars.

—SERBIAN PROVERB

It isn't just that forgiveness is like a sacred threshold or the threshing floor; like a river, a well, or an ocean; like a tiny seed or a bit of leaven. Forgiveness is both sustenance and sacrament, meant to be made and shared in community. "Bread exists to be broken, / to sustain its purpose," the Persian poet Rumi penned in the thirteenth century.[1] In its most basic form—grain ground and mixed with water—bread is one common food that unites many of us. Whether baguette or brioche, challah or ciabatta, bread connects past and present along many social, religious, and gastronomical lines.

Excavations in Egypt have unearthed ancient bakeries. Archaeological evidence has revealed that bread was used as a form

---

1. In Peck, *Bread, Body, Spirit*, 6.

of payment to those who labored on the pyramids and temples. Our ancestors all over the planet first baked their bread in the ashes of their fires; later, they built more elaborate ovens and granaries. Power was equivalent to your stores of grain in ancient Greece. In the Hebrew Bible bread often represents the social ties that bind us together as human creatures. It is an important symbol of hospitality and sign of respect.[2] *Prasadam*, or food offerings, to the Hindu gods continue to contain bread made sacred by its being offered. It is no mere coincidence that bread serves as a solid symbol for life itself, and for divine provision in this world in nearly every religion. The manna that God rained down on the hungry Israelites as they wandered through the wilderness is perhaps the quintessential manifestation of that life-sustaining promise: not only bread of life, but bread of heaven.

Yet all too often we find ourselves like Daniel Defoe's famous castaway, sure of God's intention to supply us with bread while at the same time clueless as to how to grind the grain required to make it, not to mention how to form it or bake it on our own desert island. "I believe few people have thought much," Robinson Crusoe opined in that eponymous novel, "upon the strange multitude of little things necessary in the providing, curing, dressing, making, and finishing this one article bread."[3]

Throughout the Bible, and across cultures, bread has always been so much more than bread; its sum more than its parts, more than flour stirred into water, a little bit of yeast, and maybe a pinch of salt. We can extend the metaphor into many aspects of life, including the journey we are on and whose final destination we are quickly approaching. Forgiveness is mysterious bread, indeed—a gift, like manna, from heaven. That angelic bread wasn't what the people were expecting; no butter crust or braided loaf. "What is it?" they asked. Yet, despite its strange appearance, what fell from heaven was what saved them.

---

2. See, for example, Gen 14:18; 18:6; 19:3; Deut 23:4; Ruth 2:14; 1 Sam 25:18; 28:24; and 2 Sam 16:12.

3. Defoe, *Robinson Crusoe*, 184.

The Way of the Fruitful Field

When Joni Mitchell sang, "We are stardust . . ." she wasn't only being poetic. Every element on earth was formed in the heart of some massive star. The iron that is an integral part of the blood which courses through our veins shares a common ancestry with supernovas and newly formed planets. Or as the Benedictine monk Bede Griffiths, who opened a deep and ongoing dialogue between Christianity and Hinduism wrote, "In that sense the universe is within us."[4] We are the context of our consciousness, Krishnamurti asserted; in knowing ourselves we know the universe.

Who knows how many stars there are in the Milky Way, how many grains of sand in the desert wilderness, or how many cells of yeast in the loaf of bread. The universe is not only accessible by telescope and rocket ship, but by magnifying glass and the discerning mind. Whenever we look to the night sky and spy Proxima Centauri, our nearest star other than our sun, its light will have already left that source more than four years previously. Forgiveness, when we finally catch up to it, travels as fast as light; by the time we see it, it has already been on its way to us for some time. It has, like all matter, been developing and expanding—radiating ever outward—since the beginning of space-time itself.

The Igbo of Nigeria believe that forgiveness is all around us at all times. We've only to reach out and bring it toward us. Jesus taught that we should pray "give us today our daily bread" (Matt 6:11). Before that, the Israelites were instructed to gather only enough manna to sustain them day by day. The importance of that heavenly bread is recognized, in part, in the age-old practice of setting specially baked loaves on a specially dedicated table in the temple as an offering to God.[5] Representing the twelve tribes of Israel, these loaves are called the Bread of the Presence because they are to be always in God's presence, both the table and the bread a constant reminder not only of God's promise to us, but also God's communion with us.

So too, like the Bread of the Presence, are we set on the table before the presence of God. We are manna. No need to store up;

---

4. Griffiths, *A New Vision of Reality*, 30.
5. A practice outlined in Exod 25:25–30; 35:13; 39:36; and Lev 24:5–9.

no leftovers. We have all we need. We contain the universe. We are bread and table; all-sufficient subject and place of nourishment not only for ourselves but for our brothers and sisters as well.

Baruch Atah, Adonai Elohenu, Melech Ha-Olam, Ha-Motzi Lehem Min Ha-Aretz.
Blessed are You, Lord our God, King of the Universe, who brings forth bread from the earth.

The Way of the Table

DAY THIRTY-FIVE

Woven Fine

Putting on Forgiveness

Therefore, as God's chosen people, holy and dearly loved, clothe yourselves with compassion, kindness, humility, gentleness, and patience. Bear with each other and forgive one another . . .

—COL 3:12–13A

Begin to weave and God will give you the thread.

—GERMAN PROVERB

WHILE DONNING THE APPROPRIATE clothing and footwear for making one's way through rough terrain is important, knowing when to remove those articles is just as critical. Today we put on our party clothes! We reach down and unlace our dusty, trusty hiking boots and slide them off, thanking them for bringing us this far. We remove them in order to feel the sacred ground beneath us and to practice going barefoot; having nothing between our skin and the ground of forgiveness, no heel or lace to get in the way of our dancing.

The Way of the Table

Remember God's words to Moses? "Take off your sandals, for the place where you are standing is holy ground" (Exod 3:5). Depending on which translation you read the command can also be to "remove" or "cast off your sandals." But the original word that Moses heard was more likely closer to "shed" (with all its references to metamorphosis, molting, and an animal shedding its skin) than anything else. Today we do not merely remove our old shirts of hurt and blouses of bitterness; we shed them and become that much lighter. We thought we needed those old rags to protect us from the extremes, but truth be told, they never really fit and the stitching was always coming apart at the seams from the get-go. We shed the old and useless and let it go. Free of our ill-fitting wardrobe we are transformed and translated into the boundlessly forgiving beautiful body we truly are beneath whatever trappings we happen to be wearing. We wiggle out of what once constricted us and slip into forgiveness; we sew the word into our clothes.

There was a time when those who could "dressed" for dinner. This wasn't a matter of putting on just any old thing, but of wearing the best one could afford, much like the difference between the generic word "clothing" and the nearly lost word "raiment" that some translations of the Bible use: "Is not . . . the body more than raiment?" Jesus asks in renderings of the Matthean gospel (6:25). That word is an old-fashioned one for clothing, particularly fancy clothing, and comes from an Old French word which can, in turn, be translated to mean "to adorn oneself in the very best." While the word has mostly gone out of fashion—not unlike the rare practice of getting dressed up dinner—it applies to the table at which we are about to be seated: Forgiveness is our finest attire.

We all enter the world naked. Then, before we know it, we are swaddled in blankets, bundled up in binkies, snapped up into snuggly onesies, or fitted into footie pajamas. We spend the rest of our lives covered in cloth of one kind or another, whether playing dress up or conforming to some societal dress code. "Clothes make the man," Mark Twain famously quipped, "naked people have little or no influence on society." Yet how often do we look at ourselves in the mirror, whether clothed or naked as a jaybird, and feel like the image we see reflected back to us is far from who we really are? Too often we slip into society's hand-me-downs of how to wrap ourselves in forgiveness. They're always ill-fitting—either too loose or too tight—and they never accentuate our best assets.

But every time we stand before a mirror we also have another choice: "to embrace being a creature with limits and needs, to love ourselves and those around us in all our imperfections."[1] Or, in other words, just as there is a psychology of clothing, there is a theology of dress.

The notion of the motion of putting on a garment as a way of becoming more godlike is woven throughout the New Testament. Paul, especially, makes use of the metaphor in his letters to the Colossians (as today's epigraph attests), and to the Galatians (3:27) where he equates baptism to being clothed with Christ, as well as in his second letter to the church in Corinth (5:2–3), where heaven, at least in his mind, is a garment we put on. In addition, the idea of the relic; of worshipping some article of clothing a beloved once wore, or a shred of fabric believed to have brushed up against the body of some ancient saint, has everything to do with today's proclamation that what we choose to put over our skin matters. In front of his father as well as the head of his church, St. Francis of Assisi famously shed his worldly clothing in order to put on his new habit and walk barefoot into the world. Two centuries later, Blessed Julian of Norwich would marvel that God "is our clothing who wraps us up and holds us close for love."

In Islam, those who believe and do good deeds "Allah will admit . . . to gardens beneath which rivers flow. They will be adorned therein with bracelets of gold and pearl, and their garments therein will be silk" (*The Qur'an*, al-Ḥajj 22:23). Conversely, the damned are fitted with garments of flame. Indeed, they cut for themselves such fiery clothes (22:19).

The Hebrew prophet Isaiah says that God clothes us with the garments of salvation (Isa 61:10). Sometimes, though, what we put on we also tear off: rending our garments to signify repentance, regret, anger, grief, or the desire or wish to start over. Jacob tore

---

1. Saracino, *Clothing*, 81.

at his clothes as he mourned the reported death of his son Joseph (Gen 37:34); David commanded, "Tear your clothes and gird on sackcloth and lament," when Abner, a father of Israel, was killed (2 Sam 3:31). In the book of Joel, however, God advises that we ought to be more concerned with rending our hearts, not our garments (2:13).

From the Amish or Mennonite practice of plain dress for men and women, to the Muslim practice of veiling known as *hijab*, to the customary Jewish prayer shawl or *tallit*, or Mormons who wear special undergarments, or even the Pharisees tying phylacteries containing sacred words onto their wrists or wrapping them around their foreheads, we all cloak ourselves in what we remember to be holy.

When we were young children we had to practice putting on our clothes. When we proudly tip-toed downstairs wearing socks that didn't match, or showed up at the breakfast table with our t-shirts on backwards or with tops and bottoms that complimented each other only in some yet to be discovered universe—stripes with polka dots, orange with fuchsia—our parents forgave our efforts. So too we forgive our current attire. We're just learning how to put on forgiveness, how to dress for the feast.

DAY THIRTY-SIX

Table Manners

[When] one eats in holiness, tastes the taste of food in holiness . . . the table becomes an altar.[1]

—MARTIN BUBER

It is coarse and ungraceful to throw food into the mouth as you would toss hay into a barn with a pitchfork.

—ANONYMOUS

WE ARE CALLED TO forgive one another not just by taking our seat at the unfailing table that God provides for us in the wilderness, but also by setting that table. Ultimately, we are both guest and host at the feast. We may think a feast is only about the food, but while what's on the menu and how it is prepared are key elements that go into the making of the meal, so too is the table on which we place those dishes. Just as the wilderness is an ancient and universal experience of trial and transformation, the table is an equally celebrated location of meeting and reconciliation. The very roots of English language reinforce this association. The

---

1. In Butash, *Bless This Food*, 10.

word we now know and recognize as *guest* originally referred to the common notion of welcoming the "stranger," a word that could in turn be interpreted as "enemy." In fact, the words *stranger*, *guest*, and *host* all derive from the same proto-Indo-European word *ghos-ti*, which sought to describe the reciprocity of any relationship, but especially that of hospitality.

Whether we think of ourselves as guest or host, we have already given careful attention to planning the menu of our particular feast, but there is plenty more to do in terms of preparing the table: what tablecloth will we choose? Which dishes will we place upon that cloth? Which utensils will we use? The "good" silver or the "everyday"? Should there be flowers? Candles? How will we fold the napkins? After all, not only our meal, but our very table is sacred.

We probably don't remember learning how to use a fork and knife to feed ourselves, but getting the food from our plate up to our little mouths presented a specific challenge to our still-developing fine motor skills. Especially those green peas. There were more than a few failed attempts; some mashed potatoes ended up on the floor, a noodle wiggled its way off our forks and down our shirt, but eventually we learned how to feed ourselves.

Until, that is, we went to our first fancy affair and were presented with multiple forks and spoons, and cutlery of all shapes and sizes and wondered worriedly which one to pick up first. When in doubt, we learned, simply start from the outside and work your way in. Knives and spoons will generally be on the right; forks to the left (except that tricky oyster fork that likes to be contrarian). We concern ourselves with whether or not our elbows should ever be on the table, or obsess over with which hand to correctly hold our forks. Meanwhile, I'm sure God finds the long list of table manners we've created silly and more than a bit peculiar. Which fork we use at the table set down in the wilderness doesn't really matter.

That said, how we behave at that table is paramount.

There is an oft-told traditional tale in which an angel offered an honorable man a glimpse of two similar yet very different scenarios. First, he was shown a scene at the center of which was an extravagant banquet table heaped with tantalizing fare. Yet the people seated around the table appeared emaciated, as if they had not eaten in weeks, even though plates piled high with food sat in front of each of them. "Why don't the people partake of the food?" the man wondered aloud. "Look carefully," said his guide, "and you will notice that every person at this feast has arms that cannot bend. They are unable to feed themselves." "Truly this must be hell," the man replied.

Then, the angel revealed to the man another similar scene: a festive table set with a feast, and banquet guests seated all around it. However, these people appeared to be healthy, happy, and well fed, even though it was obvious that their arms also could not bend. "I don't understand," said the man. "This looks not much different than hell." "Watch," said his guide, "and you will see there is a notable difference. In hell the people think only of feeding themselves. In heaven they have learned to feed each other."

Imagine what our world might look like if we could finally figure that out—how to feed each other, literally as well as figuratively—how to spread a table in our hearts, and add leaf after leaf to that unending table so that it might extend so far into the distance we would not be able to see its end.

While ultimately forgiveness is up to each of us individually, it is not a table for one.

DAY THIRTY-SEVEN

A Place at the Table

You prepare a table before me in the presence of my enemies . . .
—PS 23:5

You will be missed when your place at the table is empty.
—1 SAM 20:18 (NLT)

THE WORDS FROM 1 Samuel with which we begin our journey today were spoken by Jonathan to his friend David on the occasion of a very different feast than the one before us. They reveal the hatred Jonathan's father, King Saul, had for David, as well as David's true allegiance—he had chosen God over king. Later, there would be an empty seat at David's own table. His son Absalom would rebel and storm out of the house, like so many sons and daughters to this day. Sadly, that chair would remain empty, scarring David's heart grievously for the rest of his days. So too, Jonathan's tender words must have continued to ring true in David's heart, just as they reverberate in ours: "You will be missed when your place at the table is empty."

At the table of yet another Old Testament patriarch—Jacob— there was yet another empty chair, that of his daydreaming son

Joseph. The boy's eleven brothers were all seated there, but Joseph (clad in his many colored coat, a gift from his father) was gone. The ancestor who would become Israel wept over that vacancy as he understood the desperate deed his other sons had committed (Gen 37). He would not live to witness the mercy and forgiveness Joseph graciously extended to his brothers (Gen 50).

The New Testament story of the prodigal son reveals yet another chair that stood empty and waiting (Luke 15:11–32). Having received his inheritance, the rash young man bid farewell to his family, leaving behind an empty bed, an empty chair, and holes in the hearts of those who loved him. How long those places remained unfilled we are not told. But eventually, their plaintive call reached the ears of the prodigal. All the while the father waited . . . wished . . . watched. When the boy finally did appear—far off, we are told—his father ran to him. The son tried to apologize, but his father wasn't even listening; he was yelling to anyone within earshot to prepare a feast: "Quick!" he was shouting gleefully, "bring him fresh clothes and new sandals; set the table; prepare the best food; we're going to celebrate!"

Each of these empty chairs appears at first to tell a sad story. Surely they are reminders of how often and how long we choose to dwell in empty places much too desolate and hollow for the grandeur of our real spirit. Of how much time and opportunity we waste in waiting for "The Apology," or in needing to be right, or in wishing that things were different from the way they are. Those are not empty chairs waiting to be occupied, but rather empty promises that occupy us. Meanwhile, the empty chair steadfastly waits, ready for whenever we decide to get out of our own way and take our seat. The empty chair, and its corollary in a place at the table, is a rich and recurrent symbol in many cultures and religions.

Sometimes it helps to know someone has saved that seat for us. There is a medieval legend in which Jesus and his disciples gathered in Heaven to recreate the Last Supper. They waited, and waited, and waited around the table while one chair remained vacant. Finally, Judas walked in. And before there was even time for an apology, Jesus went to him and greeted him warmly, saying, "Welcome, our brother. We have been waiting for you."

While the actual tradition is to set a full glass of wine on the Passover Seder table, some Jews also uphold a long held custom of pulling up an empty chair to that feast, saving a seat for Elijah just in case the prophet shows up to herald the long-awaited coming of the Messiah.

In early Buddhist art, the figure of the Buddha is nowhere represented in human form. Instead, the blessed one appears as footprints or—more often than not—an empty chair. The reasoning behind this depiction is that emptiness best represents the unknowable, ungraspable field of being and nothingness that is the foundation of Buddhist teaching. In this way, the empty chair can be said to be a symbol of our truest nature.

Hinduism, like so many religions, has many incarnations according to the location and culture in which it developed and is practiced. For example, in Balinese Hindu temples there are often no overt images of God. Yet plenty of symbolic images abound, including that of the empty chair. Typically crafted of stone, it symbolizes, among other things, the indescribability of the divine, and always sits in homage to the High God of all Balinese Hindus: *Ida Sanghyang Widhi*, or *Acintya*—the inconceivable one, the one who cannot be imagined. In Bali, to stand in front of an empty chair is to reckon with everything you do not know and yet strive to understand.

Not only is there a place set for us at God's table, that enigmatic place is somehow constantly making room for still others to join us, to take their seat. There's no such thing as "standing room only" at God's table; there's always room for one more.

DAY THIRTY-EIGHT

The Full Cup

Then he called the bridegroom aside and said, "Everyone brings out the choice wine first and then the cheaper wine after the guests have had too much to drink; but you have saved the best till now."

—JOHN 2:9B–10

There has to be some emptying, some pouring out, if I am to make room for the new.[1]

—JOYCE RUPP

TODAY IS ABOUT THE miraculous, about multiplication, and about how the seemingly insufficient can defy the prescribed boundaries and expand into the all-encompassing: the cup. Nowhere is this symbolic container more significantly explored—especially in the context of our particular journey—than in the Twenty-third Psalm: we lack nothing, we have been guided along right paths, led by quiet waters; we lie down in green pastures. Our cup overflows.

Yet, how often do we stop to think of the ramifications of that cup having been placed on a table so lovingly prepared in the

---

1. Rupp, *The Cup of Our Life*, 2.

presence of our enemies? The question becomes, as Jesus asked the mother of Zebedee's sons: "Can you drink the cup?" (Matt 20:22). The cup is a reminder of our most basic spiritual thirst; it contains all of life's emptiness, fullness, brokenness, and blessings. Likewise, it is an integral part of every table's place setting. The cup is circular, it has no beginning or end, round and round it is a symbol of ever-expanding wholeness.

One of the first lessons in *A Course in Miracles*, a curriculum in spiritual transformation, is one about perception, about the realization that nothing is what we think it is; that everything is filtered through our beliefs, our thoughts, our memories and our experiences. In other words, that there is no such thing as immaculate perception. Wherever you are, the text says, you can look around and say to yourself, "nothing I see is what I think it is . . . that door is not a door, that table is not a table . . ." This exercise should pose no difficulty to believers everywhere, but perhaps no one more so than Christians, who gather in remembrance of another meal—the Last Supper—and understand that a cup is never just a cup; a wafer of bread so much more than a mere wafer of bread.

Over the years many traditions have evolved regarding the cup of Elijah at the Passover Seder table. Many people observe the tradition because they believe that Elijah visits everyone's table at Passover. At a certain point in the Seder a new cup of wine is poured in order to carry out, at least symbolically, the liberating opening of the Hagadah, the text recited to begin that celebration: "All those who are in need, come and eat!" At that time the faithful recount their redemption from Egypt while also expressing their hope for future redemption with the coming of the Messiah.

But the cup is not reserved only for Pesach. Every Shabbat meal begins with a blessing over a cup of wine: the Kiddush cup. Many families have a special glass or goblet, often wrought of silver and a treasured heirloom that has been lovingly passed down through the generations, used specifically for the purpose, although any cup can function as a Kiddush cup if necessary. Kiddush, or literally, "sanctification," is a blessing recited over either wine or grape juice to sanctify the moment. Significantly, after the person reciting the Kiddush drinks from the cup, it is passed around the table or poured out into smaller cups for the other participants.

In the Christian tradition the cup is the vessel, the chalice, the actual Holy Grail which Jesus used at the Last Supper. That tradition's eucharistic celebration honors the original elements of that ultimate feast: the bread and the "cup" or chalice, with the celebrant using the words of Jesus as recorded by the gospel writers Matthew (26:27–29), Mark (14:23–24) and Luke (22:20), as well as the Apostle Paul (1 Corinthians): "this is my blood of the new covenant, which is poured out for many for the forgiveness of sins." Saint John of Chrysostom asserted, in the fourth century, that just as that table was not silver, neither was that chalice gold; yet everything there was just as precious.

We too often compare every bit of our lives with the bits and pieces of others, trying to decide whether we are better or worse off. But such comparisons do not help us much. "We have to live our life, not someone else's," the Catholic priest Henri Newman wrote, "We have to hold our own cup."[2] Just as cups are containers designed to hold the divine, so too are we meant to be containers of that which is beyond our human capacity to hold.

Ultimately, the cup is about thirst. This is no joke, but if it were we might imagine that an English clergyman, an imam, a French Jesuit, a rabbi, a Hindu pandit, and a Buddhist walked into a bar, each noticing a full glass on the bar top. The Englishman said, "That is a chalice." The imam answered, "No, it is a *finjan*." The French Jesuit commented, "Your dictionaries must both be wrong; *il s'agit d'une tasse*." The rabbi said, "What do I know from '*tasse*'? This is a *qubbaath*, a Kiddush cup." The Brahmin priest politely corrected, "No, I believe what you see before you is a *jāma*." Just then the Buddhist bellied up to the bar, drank from the cup, and after he drank said, "Whatever you call it; it is meant to be drunk—stop your semantics and quench your thirsts!"

---

2. Nouwen, *Can You Drink the Cup?*, 31.

DAY THIRTY-NINE

Soul Food

The Pantry of Forgiveness

Salt is good, but if it loses its saltiness, how can you make it salty again? Have salt among yourselves, and be at peace with each other.

—MARK 9:50

Whether it is roast lamb and bitter herbs served at a Passover meal, lentil soup and fig cakes eaten at the end of a day of fasting during Ramadan, or the bread and wine Christians partake of when they gather to observe the Lord's Supper, food for the body also becomes food for the soul.[1]

—MARLENE KROPF

SINCE WE ARE BOTH guest and host at the table, and forgiveness is the soul food we share at the feast, it is vital that we also understand how best to prepare and serve this meal: the virtues of the slow simmer and fine cooking. If food for the body is truly food for the soul, then we must cultivate not only our capacity to host and serve; we must also hone our skills in the kitchen of

---

1. Kropf in Yoder et al., *Preparing Sunday Dinner*, 22.

forgiveness. We consume every day proteins, carbohydrates, fats, minerals, fiber, and vitamins in order to thrive. Just as those primary ingredients of physical health ensure our ability to survive, so too there are correlative ingredients that guarantee our spiritual well-being—elements that comprise the recipe for forgiveness. The well-stocked pantry of forgiveness contains curiosity, openness, awareness, empathy, intention, mercy, grace—along with a veritable cupboard full of flavorful spices and intriguing seasonings that flavor our lives.

As newborns, we needed to be fed every few hours; we were completely dependent on others for the timing, quality, and quantity of the sustenance we received. Eventually we learned to get food into our hungry mouths all on our own—given that it was put in front of us—and we learned how to feed ourselves. Over time we developed our own unique food preferences and styles of eating. Ultimately, everything about what we chose to be life-sustaining became our own decision, regardless of whether or not those choices also fed our souls. In other words, we learned to either fast or feast: to feed or appease our anger, gorge ourselves on discouragement or fill ourselves with hope, abstain from worry or trust, refrain from bitter resentment or feast on forgiveness. We all know there are certain health benefits to eating the right foods every day. While the cupboard of forgiveness remains a daily option, more often than not we sadly opt to stay out of the kitchen altogether and choose instead to rifle through the filing cabinet of past grievances.

While ultimately God, by whatever name, is the source of the soul food we each so desperately need in order for our spirit to thrive, it is up to us to make healthy choices all around—to pay careful attention to how we are feeding our self not only physically, but also mentally, emotionally, and spiritually. What kind of nutrition does our soul really get from resentment or revenge? It may be fast food, and satisfy a certain craving, but is it really good for us? The American writer and theologian Frederick Buechner noted the certain appeal that such fast foods embody at the surface: "to lick your wounds, to smack your lips over grievances long past . . . to savor to the last toothsome morsel both the pain you are given and the pain you are giving back," and the reality beneath all the temptation: "The chief drawback is that what you are wolfing down is yourself. The skeleton at the feast is you."[2]

There is a big difference between eating to survive and savoring each bite of a decadent meal. It is entirely possible to eat without thinking, but should we? Likewise, cooking can be seen as a necessary daily task or an everyday experiment in trying out new flavors—drudgery or discovery. We can choose to either "fix it and forget it," or pay careful attention to the process. They say, "the watched pot will never boil." Forgiveness cannot be rushed, but neither can it be overcooked, while, conversely, the unwatched pot of lingering resentment always risks boiling over.

There are plenty of foods that may be good for us but make us turn up our noses nonetheless. Spinach is still spinach no matter how you prepare it. Let's face it; forgiveness (not to mention its usual side dishes) is not always easy to swallow. While we may crave its smooth flavor, not all its ingredients may be to our taste: "Maybe forgiveness is the Limburger cheese of human affairs," the psychologist and forgiveness researcher Robert Enright noted, "at first it seems offensive, so offensive that we dare not try it."[3] Perhaps the book of Job advises best: "Can that which is unsavory be eaten without salt?" (6:6). Sometimes we need something else to make the flavor of what's on our fork a little more palatable: the salt of courage, perhaps, or even the seasoning of compassion. All three of the Synoptic Gospels speak about the goodness of salt (Matt 5:13; Mark 9:50; Luke 14:34). Paul admonished that our words should always be "full of grace" and "seasoned with salt" (Col 4:6). Salt is mentioned so often in the Bible it's tempting to say that whoever the saints and prophets went to for their annual physical would have looked up from their blood pressure readings and quickly prescribed a low-sodium diet. But each of them was employing in their own way salt as a metaphor for a certain kind of careful thought or wisdom.

    2. Buechner, *Wishful Thinking*, 2.
    3. Enright, *Forgiveness Is a Choice*, 23.

Soul Food

As offensive as forgiveness may sometimes first appear to our palate, once we try it we might just find we like the flavor, that its seasonings, in fact, need no adjustment. It's hard to say what forgiveness tastes like, but once we do get a taste of the strange substance we often want more. Somewhere beyond the four basic building blocks of all flavors—sweet, sour, salty, and bitter—forgiveness is like that subtle and indescribable so-called fifth taste (known as umami) that expands and rounds out the other four and just makes everything taste better.

At special meals, family celebrations, and holiday dinners we pay more attention to planning the menu and preparing the meal. We choose an entrée—the main course—and then shape the rest of the meal around it, giving extra thought about what dishes would best complement the entrée and honor the day. Today, forgiveness is at the center of our sacred meal. What goes best with forgiveness? Some of the same things that went into preparing it: the side dishes we remember from our childhood, like curiosity, but also more recently acquired tastes like wisdom and humility, not to mention patience and time, but most of all the gravy of thanksgiving. Just as all eucharistic worship can be said to be both an ordinary dinner as well as a foretaste of an even greater feast to come, forgiveness is appetizer as well as entrée at the same time, and somehow even dessert—a foretaste of something even greater, sweeter, better . . .

There's plenty more where it comes from. Help yourself.

DAY FORTY

The Gift of Forgiveness

And he took bread, gave thanks . . .
—LUKE 22:19

If my hands are occupied with holding on to anything, then they are not capable of either giving or receiving.[1]
—DOROTHEE SOËLLE

AFTER THE SOWING AND the reaping, the threshing and the winnowing, the planning and cooking and baking, the pressing of the tablecloth, and the setting of the table . . . comes time for the meal. All that's left is grace—in whatever form it may take. It is forbidden to taste any of the pleasures of this world, the Talmud reminds us, without some kind of blessing.

God is always giving: promised land, manna from heaven, water from stone, breath to dirt, light in the dark, strength in adversity . . . even Jesus amongst us (John 3:16). What matters is our posture, the manner in which we arrange our hands; whether we accept or reject the gifts extended to us. God reached out and

---

1. Soëlle, *The Strength of the Weak*, 33.

touched Jeremiah's lips and said, "I have put my words in your mouth" (Jer 1:9). Ezekiel was given an entire scroll of God's words with which to fill his stomach, and both prophets swallowed those words. They "tasted sweet as honey" (Ezek 3:1–4). But neither of those divine meals was complete only in the tasting; each prophet was not only to receive that manna, but to give it, share it—speak it forward—to others.

Conversely, we are forever putting words into each other's mouths, (mis-)interpreting what someone says so that the words mean what we want them to mean and not necessarily what the speaker originally intended. From political attack ads to the dynamics of a family disagreement, plenty of examples abound. The graphic turn of phrase even has biblical roots. Joab, a captain in King David's army (albeit because his mother Zeruiah was the monarch's sister), intentionally and deceptively put words into the mouth of a widow from Tekoa: "Pretend you are in mourning," he instructed, "Then go to the king and speak these words to him." And Joab put the words in her mouth (2 Sam 14:2–3).

But there are words that are all our own, words we very much mean and want to say. Jesus took the bread and, understanding it was a gift, said thanks. And then he shared it with those around him. So, too, are we called to take, to bless, to break, to give. The word on our lips is meant to be spoken, to be shared—to become more than a series of letters, vowels, consonants, and syllables on the page—embodied: the word become flesh. If forgiveness is a gift, it is only a gift if we receive it. And somehow part of receiving that gift is also giving it away. "If I cease to take and give, I become a stone . . .," the German theologian Dorothee Soëlle prefaced her words that stand as an epigraph for today's meditation. Her theology revolved around equality and emphasized values such as reciprocity and mutuality, and thus found the saying "It is more blessed to give than to receive" profoundly misleading and inherently one-sided. "Perhaps we should say instead," she concluded, "It is more blessed to give *and* receive than to have and hold."[2] In open-handedly receiving the gift of forgiveness, we become a gift

---

2. Ibid, emphasis added.

to others. If there is no give and take, then we prevent forgiveness from showing up anywhere at all.

Of all the gifts that grace our lives people are the most precious. Whether we eagerly await them, like a gaily wrapped present on our birthday, or they show up unexpectedly and in a different sort of wrapping altogether, every gift—including our self—deserves not only our attention but also our appreciation. No strings attached. People often come wrapped in multiple layers. However they arrive in our lives, whether wrapped in anger, camouflaged in the constant need to be right, or draped with doubt and distancing distrust, we need not tear into them but open the gift they are carefully. "Life is so generous a giver," Fra Giovanni observed in the fourteenth century, "but we, judging its gifts by the covering, cast them away as ugly, or heavy, or hard. Remove the covering and you will find beneath it a living splendor, woven of love, by wisdom, with power."[3] The past is not the root of all our troubles, but rather the dusty road that delivered us here to this sacred moment in our present lives.

These days, it is not difficult to come upon the popular maxim: "forgiveness is a gift." Dig only ever-so-slightly below that surface and it becomes clear that the gift in consideration is a present we give to ourselves. Or, in other words, that when we forgive others we give ourselves the gift of emotional liberation. All of which is ever so important and true. But we toss these phrases around willy-nilly, without acknowledging who the ultimate Giver is. We do ourselves a disservice if we believe that the generosity of spirit that brings forgiveness to us in the first place stops there. If forgiveness is a gift to ourselves, from Whom do we ultimately receive it? And if it is a gift, it is only a gift if we, in fact, receive it—take it—from Wherever it comes from, only to then pass it on; give it away.

---

3. While the Italian friar and scholar, Giovanni Giocondo, (ca. 1433–1515) is often identified as the author of these words from the widely quoted, "A Letter to the Most Illustrious the Contessina Allagia degli Aldobrandeschi, Written Christmas Eve Anno Domino 1513," more recent scholarship finds the authorship of that letter to be uncertain.

The Gift of Forgiveness

We are called not only to receive the blessing, but to be the blessing. "When we bless, we are enabled somehow to go beyond our present frontiers and reach into the source," O'Donohue wrote, "a blessing awakens future wholeness."[4] And a blessing is not simply some ideal, some random collection of words we recite by rote and to which we aspire, but an action, a verb—something physical, something we do; an action that not only keeps our awareness of life's holiness ever-present, but also extends the boundaries of the sacred. Not only has science proved the process of forgiving to have certain health benefits—lowering our blood pressure as well as our levels of cortisol, the steroid hormone our bodies release in response to stress—so too the act of blessing has been shown to improve our quality of life. In fact, when we forgive not only because we believe it is "good for us," but because we truly desire to extend a blessing to our offender as well, the proven health benefits of forgiveness multiply exponentially.[5]

We may be guest and host at the table, the choice of whether to serve and taste forgiveness may be up to each of us individually; but still (and before all that) there is the miraculous gift of the table set before us. It doesn't just appear in the wilderness. The fact that we are suddenly aware of forgiveness, that we have it to give and receive, is the real gift. Today we stop and consider from where— and more importantly from Whom—our feast comes from; that forgiveness can be simultaneously a welcome feast for us, a meal that we share with others, and a banquet in honor of the One who provided that feast.

The table is set. Everything is ready.

---

4. O'Donohue, *To Bless the Space*, 198.
5. See Worthington., *Forgiving and Reconciling.*

AFTERWORD

We Live to Forgive

"Seek and you will find," the Gospels assure.¹ Yet, hopefully, our journey has shown us that the finding is not nearly as important as the seeking. In the second logion of the Gospel of Thomas, Jesus reminds all seekers that finding is not the ultimate end; that astonishment and marvel always await beyond arrival.² In other words, it isn't about the worship, but the work; not the destination, but the process. This is our rightful heritage.

Ultimately, the feast of forgiveness is something we participate in; a meal meant to be savored, not some event to be marked on the calendar and then crossed off a list. It's a never-ending feast, to be at table with each other: something we not only attend but attend to. Its greatest secret is that it is really everywhere, offered to us at every moment and wherever we find ourselves. In a very real way there is no journey through the wilderness at all. Any movement from one location to another takes place within the few short inches of our boundless hearts. Forgiveness is not something we find, but live; not an action but a way. Ultimately we do not learn how to forgive; we *live* how to forgive.

If we have learned anything on this journey, it is that forgiveness is a way: a way through the wilderness; a way of opening

---

1. An instruction that appears in both Matthew (7:7), and Luke (11:9).
2. "Yeshua said: 'Whoever searches must continue to search until they find. When they find, they will be disturbed; and being disturbed, they will marvel and will reign over all'" (NHC II, 2).

AFTERWORD

doors; a way of putting one foot in front of the other; a way of seeing things as they truly are; a way of not only feeling, but knowing with our hearts; a way of flowing like all water to its source; a way of planting and tending holy ground; a way of harvesting sacred fruits and setting the table for the ultimate feast. It isn't just that forgiveness is like a holy threshold, like a mirror, like a dusty road or a meandering river, like leaven or a tiny seed. The door, the path, the heart, our eyes, our feet, all contain some lesson of forgiveness for us to learn.

"The risen Christ makes life a perpetual feast," said Saint Athanasius. So too forgiveness ever rises, like the grain resurrected in the loaf of bread; like when we are seated at a wonderful table and we hope the party will never end. For us, this is the end of our forty-day journey. But it is really just the beginning: "[God's] compassions never fail; they are new every morning" (Lam 3:22b–23a).

In our beginning was the door. And in that door is the table.

Always.

Bibliography

Arendt, Hannah. *The Human Condition*. Chicago: University of Chicago Press, 1998.
Augustine. *The Confessions*. Translated by Maria Boulding. San Francisco: Ignatius, 2012.
Bach, Richard. *Illusions: The Adventures of a Reluctant Messiah*. New York: Delacorte, 1977.
Bachelard, Gaston. *The Poetics of Space*. Translated by Maria Jolas. Boston: Beacon, 1969.
Baker, Isaac Newton. *An Intimate View of Robert G. Ingersoll*. New York: C. P. Farrell, 1920.
Battle, Michael *Ubuntu: I in You and You in Me*. New York: Seabury, 2009.
Bangley, Bernard. *By Way of the Desert: 365 Daily Readings*. Brewster, MA: Paraclete, 2007.
Barks, Coleman, ed. *The Essential Rumi*. New York: HarperCollins, 2010.
Barnes, Christopher. *Boris Pasternak: A Literary Biography*. Vol. 2. Cambridge: Cambridge University Press, 2004.
Batterson, Mark. *Wild Goose Chase: Reclaiming the Adventure of Pursuing God*. Colorado Springs: Multnomah, 2008.
Berra, Yogi, and Dave Kaplan. *When You Come to a Fork in the Road, Take It! Inspiration and Wisdom from One of Baseball's Greatest Heroes*. New York: Hyperion, 2001.
Beston, Henry. "The St. Lawrence." In *Dark Waters Dancing to a Breeze: A Literary Companion to Rivers and Lakes*, edited by Wayne Grady, 64–69. Vancouver: Greystone, 2007.
Blake, William. *The Complete Poetry and Prose of William Blake*. Edited by D. V. Erdman. Berkeley: University of California Press, 2008.
Brudholm, Thomas, and Thomas Cushman, eds. *The Religious in Response to Mass Atrocity: Interdisciplinary Perspectives*. New York: Cambridge University Press, 2009.
Buechner, Frederick *The Sacred Journey: A Memoir of Early Days*. New York: HarperCollins, 1982.
———. *Wishful Thinking: A Theological ABC*. New York: Harper & Row, 1973.

Bibliography

Butash, Adrian. *Bless This Food: Ancient and Contemporary Graces from Around the World*. Novato, CA: New World, 2007.
Campbell, Joseph. *Pathways to Bliss: Mythology and Personal Transformation*. The Collected Works of Joseph Campbell. Novato, CA: New World, 2004.
Carroll, Lewis. *Alice in Wonderland and Through the Looking-Glass*. New York: Barnes & Noble, 2012.
Carter, Alexandra, ed. *The Routledge Dance Studies Reader*. New York: Routledge, 1998.
Chang, Larry, ed. *Wisdom for the Soul: Five Millennia of Prescriptions for Spiritual Healing*. Washington, DC: Gnosophia, 2006.
Chesterton, Gilbert Keith. *Orthodoxy*. Hollywood: Simon & Brown, 2012.
Crothers, R. McChord. *Ralph Waldo Emerson: How to Know Him*. Indianapolis: Bobbs-Merrill, 1921.
Defoe, Daniel. *Robinson Crusoe*. New York: Aladdin, 2001.
Dickinson, Emily. *The Complete Poems of Emily Dickinson*. Edited by Thomas H. Johnson. New York: Little, Brown, 1961.
Dossey, Barbara Montgomery, et al. *Florence Nightingale Today: Healing, Leadership, Global Action*. Silver Spring, MD: American Nurses Association, 2005.
Eliot, T. S. *The Annotated* Waste Land *with Eliot's Contemporary Prose*. Edited by Lawrence S. Rainey. New Haven: Yale University Press, 2006.
Enright, Robert D. *Forgiveness Is a Choice: A Step-by-Step Process for Resolving Anger and Restoring Hope*. Washington, DC: APA LifeTools, 2001.
Evans, Alice. "Leaning into the Light: An Interview with Barry Lopez." *Poets and Writers* 22 (March/April 1994) 62–79.
Fitzhenry, Robert I., ed. *The Harper Book of Quotations*. New York: HarperCollins, 1993.
Ford, Marcia. *The Sacred Art of Forgiveness: Forgiving Ourselves and Others through God's Grace*. Woodstock, VT: SkyLight Paths, 2006.
Frost, Robert. *The Poetry of Robert Frost: The Collected Poems, Complete and Unabridged*. Edited by Edward Connery Latham. New York: Henry Holt, 1969.
Geisel, Theodor Seuss *Oh, the Places You'll Go!* New York: Random House, 1988.
Gerber, Charles R. *Healing for a Bitter Heart: Releasing the Power of Forgiveness*. Joplin, MO: College Press, 1996.
Gibran, Kahlil. *The Kahlil Gibran Reader: Inspirational Writings*. New York: Kensington, 2006.
Green, Arthur. *These Are the Words: A Vocabulary of Jewish Spiritual Life*. Woodstock, VT: Jewish Lights, 2012.
Griffiths, Bede. *A New Vision of Reality: Western Science, Eastern Mysticism and Christian Faith*. Springfield, IL: Templegate, 1989.
Harvey, Andrew *The Direct Path: Creating a Journey to the Divine through the World's Mystical Traditions*. New York: Broadway, 2000.
———. *Teachings of the Christian Mystics*. Boston: Shambhala, 1998.

BIBLIOGRAPHY

———. *The Way of Passion: A Celebration of Rumi.* Berkeley: Frog, 1994.
Heschel, Abraham Joshua. *God in Search of Man: A Philosophy of Judaism.* New York: Farrar, Straus & Giroux, 1976.
———. *The Wisdom of Heschel.* Translated by Ruth M. Goodhill. New York: Macmillan, 1986.
Hogan, Linda "Walking." *Parabola* 15/2 (1990) 14–16.
Hong, Howard Vincent, and Edna Hatlestad Hong, eds. *The Essential Kierkegaard.* Princeton: Princeton University Press, 2000.
Hopkins, Jeffrey, ed. *The Art of Peace: Nobel Peace Laureates Discuss Human Rights, Conflict and Reconciliation.* Ithaca, NY: Snow Lion, 2000.
Iacoboni, Marco. *Mirroring People: The Science of Empathy and How We Connect with Others.* New York: Farrar, Straus & Giroux, 2009.
Ibn al-'Arabi. *The Bezels of Wisdom.* Translated by R. W. J. Austin. New York: Paulist, 1980.
Kamath, M. V. *Gandhi: A Spiritual Journey.* Mumbai: Indus Source, 2007.
Keller, David G. R. *Desert Banquet: A Year of Wisdom from the Desert Mothers and Fathers.* Collegeville, MN: Liturgical, 2011.
———. *Oasis of Wisdom: The Words of the Desert Fathers and Mothers.* Collegeville, MN: Liturgy, 2005.
Kidd, Sue Monk. *The Secret Life of Bees.* New York: Penguin, 2003.
King, Martin Luther King, Jr. *A Call to Conscience: The Landmark Speeches of Dr. Martin Luther King Jr.* Edited by Clayborne Carson and Kris Shepard. New York: Warner, 2001.
Kingsolver, Barbara. *The Poisonwood Bible.* New York: HarperCollins, 1998.
Krutch, Joseph Wood. *The Desert Year.* New York: William Sloane, 1952.
Kushner, Lawrence. *Honey from the Rock: An Easy Introduction to Jewish Mysticism.* Woodstock, VT: Jewish Lights, 2000.
L'Amour, Louis. *Ride the Dark Trail.* New York: Random House, 1972.
Lane, Belden C. *The Solace of Fierce Landscapes: Exploring Desert and Mountain Spirituality.* New York: Oxford University Press, 1998.
Lewis, C. S. *Mere Christianity.* New York: HarperCollins, 2001.
Lionberger, John. *Renewal in the Wilderness: A Spiritual Guide to Connecting with God in the Natural World.* Woodstock, VT: SkyLight Paths, 2007.
Machado, Antonio. *Border of a Dream: Selected Poems of Antonio Machado.* Translated by Willis Barnstone. Port Townsend, WA: Copper Canyon, 2003.
———. *There Is No Road.* Translated by Mary G. Berg and Dennis Maloney. Buffalo: White Pines, 2003.
Maclean, Norman. *A River Runs Through It and Other Stories.* Chicago: University of Chicago Press, 1976.
May, Gerald. *The Wisdom of Wilderness: Experiencing the Healing Power of Nature.* New York: HarperCollins, 2006.
McLaren, Brian D. *Finding Our Way Again: The Return of the Ancient Practices.* Nashville: Thomas Nelson, 2008.
Merton, Thomas. *The Seven Storey Mountain.* New York: Harcourt, Brace, 1948.

Miller, James. *Thoughts from Earth: A Book of Gentle Wisdom*. Bloomington, IN: Trafford, 2004.
Milton, John. *Paradise Lost*. Edited by David Scott Kastan. Indianapolis: Hackett, 2005.
Mirren, Helen. "Helen Mirren: I Still Have a Gypsy Sense of Adventure." Interview by Tim Adams. *The Guardian*, 2011. http://www.theguardian.com/film/2011/sep/25/helen-mirren-the-debt-interview.
Morrow, Susan Brind. *The Names of Things: Life, Language, and Beginnings in the Egyptian Desert*. New York: Riverhead, 1997.
Nomura, Yushi. *Desert Wisdom: Sayings from the Desert Fathers*. Garden City, NY: Doubleday 1982.
Nouwen, Henri. *Can You Drink the Cup?* Notre Dame: Ave Maria, 2006.
O'Donohue, John. *Beauty: The Invisible Embrace*. New York: HarperCollins, 2004.
———. *Four Elements: Reflections on Nature*. New York: Harmony, 2010.
———. *To Bless the Space Between Us: A Book of Blessings*. New York: Doubleday, 2008.
O'Grady, Selina, and John Wilkins, eds. *Great Spirits 1000–2000: The Fifty-Two Christians Who Most Influenced Their Millennium*. Mahwah, NJ: Paulist, 2002.
Peck, Alice, ed. *Bread, Body, Spirit: Finding the Sacred in Food*. Woodstock, VT: SkyLight Paths, 2008.
Proust, Marcel. *Remembrance of Things Past*. Translated by C. K. Scott-Moncreiff. Hertfordshire, UK: Wordsworth, 2006.
Richardson, Jan L. *Night Visions: Searching the Shadows of Advent and Christmas*. Cleveland: United Church, 1998.
Rilke, Rainer Maria. *Letters to a Young Poet*. Translated by Stephen Mitchell. New York: Vintage, 1984.
Rowling, J. K. *Harry Potter and the Sorcerer's Stone*. New York: Levine, 1997.
Ruggiero, Vincent Ryan. *Making Your Mind Matter: Strategies for Increasing Practical Intelligence*. Lanham, MD: Rowman & Littlefield, 2003.
Rupp, Joyce. *The Cup of Our Life: A Guide to Spiritual Growth*. Notre Dame: Ave Maria, 1997.
Saint-Exupéry, Antoine de. *The Little Prince*. Translated by Richard Howard. New York: Harcourt, 2000.
Samuels, M. A. "The Brain–Heart Connection." *Circulation: Journal of the American Heart Association* 116 (2007) 77–84. doi: 10.1161/CIRCULATIONAHA.106.678995.
Saracino, Michele. *Clothing*. Minneapolis: Fortress, 2012.
Shlain, Leonard. *The Alphabet Versus the Goddess: The Conflict Between Word and Image*. New York: Viking, 1998.
Soëlle, Dorothee. *The Strength of the Weak: Toward a Christian Feminist Identity*. Translated by Robert Kimber and Rita Kimber. Philadelphia: Westminster, 1984.

Bibliography

Talbot, John Michael. *The Lessons of St. Francis: How to Bring Simplicity and Spirituality into Your Daily Life.* New York: Dutton, 1997.

Taylor, Barbara Brown. *An Altar in the World: A Geography of Faith.* New York: HarperOne, 2009.

Taylor, Laini. *Daughter of Smoke and Bone.* London: Hodder & Stoughton, 2011.

Teilhard de Chardin, Pierre. *Toward the Future.* New York: Harcourt, 1973.

Thoreau, Henry David. *Walden.* New York: Holt, Rinehart & Winston, 1963.

———. *Walking.* New York: HarperCollins, 1994.

Tolkien, J. R. R. *The Fellowship of the Ring: The Lord of the Rings.* New York: Ballantine, 1994.

———. *The Return of the King.* Boston: Houghton Mifflin, 1965.

Tournier, Paul. *Creative Suffering.* New York: HarperCollins, 1983.

Tutu, Desmond. *No Future Without Forgiveness.* New York: Doubleday, 1999.

Wiederkehr, Macrina. *Abide: Keeping Vigil with the Word of God.* Collegeville, MN: Liturgical, 2011.

Worthington, Everett L. *Forgiving and Reconciling: Bridges to Wholeness and Hope.* Downers Grove, IL: Intervarsity, 2001.

Yoder, June Alliman, et al. *Preparing Sunday Dinner: A Collaborative Approach to Worship and Preaching.* Scottdale, PA: Herald, 2005.

Zusak, Markus. *The Book Thief.* New York: Knopf, 2007.

www.ingramcontent.com/pod-product-compliance
Lightning Source LLC
Chambersburg PA
CBHW050804160426
43192CB00010B/1631